Understanding ESOPs

2020 UPDATE

Corey Rosen
Scott Rodrick

The National Center for Employee Ownership
Oakland, California

Visit us at **www.nceo.org** for more information about ESOPs

This publication is designed to provide accurate and authoritative information in regard to the subject matter covered. It is sold with the understanding that the publisher is not engaged in rendering legal, accounting, or other professional service. If legal advice or other expert assistance is required, the services of a competent professional person should be sought.

Legal, accounting, and other rules affecting business often change. Before making decisions based on the information you find here or in any publication from any publisher, you should ascertain what changes might have occurred and what changes might be forthcoming. The NCEO's website (including the members-only resources) and newsletter for members provide regular updates on these changes. If you have any questions or concerns about a particular issue, check with your professional advisor or, if you are an NCEO member, call or email us.

Understanding ESOPs, 2020 Update
Corey Rosen and Scott Rodrick

Book design by Scott Rodrick

Copyright © 2008, 2013, 2014, 2016, 2018, 2020 by The National Center for Employee Ownership. All rights reserved. Printed in the United States of America. No part of this book may be reproduced or transmitted in any form or by any means, electronic or mechanical, including photocopying, recording, or by any information storage and retrieval system, without prior written permission from the publisher.

First published in 2008; reprinted in 2013, 2014, 2016, 2018, and 2020 with updates.

ISBN: 978-1-938220-84-5

The National Center for Employee Ownership
1629 Telegraph Ave., Suite 200
Oakland, CA 94612
Phone (510) 208-1300
Website: www.nceo.org

Contents

Preface   v

1. An Overview of How ESOPs Work   1
Corey Rosen

2. Selling to an ESOP in a Closely Held Company   27
Scott Rodrick

3. ESOPs in S Corporations   43
Corey Rosen

4. Things to Do with an ESOP Besides Buying Out the Owner   59
Corey Rosen

5. Understanding ESOP Valuation   71
Corey Rosen

6. Financing an ESOP   99
Corey Rosen

7. ESOP Distribution and Diversification Rules   119
Scott Rodrick

8. Choosing Consultants and Trustees   137
Corey Rosen

9. ESOPs, Corporate Performance, and Ownership Culture   145
Corey Rosen

About the Authors   165

About the NCEO   166

Preface

When the National Center for Employee Ownership (NCEO) was founded in 1981, employee ownership was a relatively unknown and somewhat suspect notion. Today, we estimate that more than 30 million Americans own stock in their companies through one kind of plan or another. More than 14 million are participants in an employee stock ownership plan (ESOP), the subject of this book.

The first chapter of this book presents an overview of what ESOPs are, how they work, and what they are used for. Subsequent chapters delve into important topics that deserve more detailed treatment. Finally, the last chapter discusses how an ESOP can improve corporate performance and how that is linked to creating an ownership culture.

This book is for the reader who desires a general overview of the subject. There are many other issues, however, and beyond that there are other equity plans that can be used in addition to or instead of an ESOP. For more information on plan feasibility, technical matters, communicating to employees, creating an ownership culture, using other equity plans, and other matters, see our more than 60 publications as well as our vast array of other informational resources at www.nceo.org.

2020 Update

This book was originally published in 2008 and then updated in various respects for the 2013, 2014, 2016, and 2018 printings. In the 2020 printing, the old chapter on valuation has been replaced with a newly updated discussion of how valuation works in an ESOP context. The chapter on choosing consultants was extensively rewritten to address contemporary situations and concerns more clearly. In addition, other routine clarifications and updates were made throughout the book (for example, at the end of 2019 the SECURE Act increased the age 70½ threshold for minimum required distributions to 72, so the chapter on distributions was updated accordingly).

Chapter 1

An Overview of How ESOPs Work

Corey Rosen

For many business owners, sharing ownership with employees just makes sense. If employees are focused on the same goals as the owners, the business will perform better and everyone will be better off. An employee stock ownership plan (ESOP) is a specific way to share ownership with employees that can provide tax benefits to the company, to sellers of stock to an ESOP, and to employees. The most common use of an ESOP is for business transition. Business owners selling to an ESOP also often see this approach as the best way to preserve the company's legacy, reward the people who helped build the business, and provide options for the owners to remain in the business in a capacity they choose. Congress has made this more appealing by providing sellers and companies with generous tax incentives for sales to qualifying ESOPs, making this kind of transition financially competitive or better in all but a small percentage of cases. Other business owners are not looking to sell, but want to reward employees with a stake in the company and help create or reinforce a culture in which employees think and act like owners. ESOPs are also used to acquire other companies, to spin off subsidiaries or divisions, and to finance capital growth. For all their many benefits, ESOPs are not right for every company. Whatever the objective, ESOPs are an important option to consider.

Given statutory authority in 1974 under the Employee Retirement Income Security Act (ERISA), ESOPs are governed by many of the same rules that cover 401(k) plans, deferred profit-sharing plans, pension plans, and other retirement plans. Unlike these other plans, however, only ESOPs are designed to invest primarily in the stock of the employer, and only ESOPs can borrow money. ESOPs should not be confused with employee stock option plans, which are covered by a very different set of rules. Nor are ESOPs to be confused with stock purchase plans. In fact, ESOPs are almost always funded by the company, not by employee contributions.

The basic concept of an ESOP is simple. A company sets up a trust fund to acquire and hold company stock. The company can contribute shares directly, contribute cash to buy shares, or have the trust borrow money to buy stock, with the company repaying the loan through contributions to the plan. The company also can contribute cash to the trust or pay dividends or distributions on shares held by the trust. The shares, and any other contributions, are allocated to employee accounts based on an equitable formula. Companies cannot, however, make allocations based on discretionary approaches, such as performance assessments. Employees acquire vesting rights to these allocations over time. After employees terminate, their account balances are distributed to them, with some exceptions described below. The plan is governed by a trustee, normally appointed by the company's board of directors; the minimum allowable governance rights for employees are very limited, although some companies provide more extensive ones. Within broad limits, contributions to the plan are tax-deductible. Employees pay no tax on what is in their accounts until they actually receive a distribution, and even then they can roll the distribution into an IRA or other retirement plan. Some sellers to an ESOP can defer capital gains taxes on the sale, and the profits attributable to the ESOP in an S corporation are not taxable at the federal and, usually, state levels.

For all their many benefits, ESOPs are not right for every company. They are more complex than other retirement plans, they do not allow as much flexibility as less tax-favored approaches to sharing ownership, and they usually are a poor fit for extremely small companies (typically with fewer than 10 to 15 employees) and companies that either are not or do not soon anticipate making a profit.

This book is written for people thinking about ESOPs. It walks you through the various rules and applications, discusses what to think about in setting up a plan, and provides guidance on how to make the plan work well for your company. As an introduction to the topic, it is not meant to be comprehensive. The NCEO does, however, have a variety of detailed publications on ESOP applications, tax issues, administrative practices, and ownership culture. For a list, go to our website at www.nceo.org.

This chapter provides a broad overview of ESOPs. Subsequent chapters look at ESOP applications and rules in more detail, while a final chapter discusses what may be the most important potential benefit of an ESOP, namely the potential to create a more engaged and productive culture.

The Development of ESOPs

ESOPs were created in the 1950s by Louis Kelso, an investment banker and attorney in San Francisco. Kelso was looking for a practical way to address what he saw as a looming problem: changes in technology and capital investment were going to eliminate many good-paying jobs, and people would increasingly face stagnating wages. In contrast, the 1% of the population who owned most of the wealth would see their fortunes soar. Kelso was seen either as a prophet or a crank at the time, but he turned out to be absolutely prescient.

Kelso's solution was to create a way for workers to share in ownership, not just get wages. If more workers were capital owners, they would have an additional source of wealth besides what they could save from wages. Of course, workers couldn't easily become capitalists by buying stock precisely because their wages were stagnating, while their perceived and real consumption needs were growing, pushing savings rates down. The trick was how to encourage business owners to share ownership in their companies with employees. Part of that was convincing them that doing so would make their companies more productive, but a larger part would need to come from financial incentives.

> ### The Windings Story
>
> Windings is a New Ulm, Minnesota, manufacturer of custom-built electric motors. It has over 100 employees. Here is what Roger Ryberg, the former owner of Windings, told us about why he decided an ESOP worked for him:
>
> *I was drawn to the ESOP idea because employee ownership seemed like a win-win-win: a win for the owner, the employees, and for the community. Private equity or a third-party sale would take away our independence without the employees reaping potential reward.*
>
> *So a little over 10 years after I started exploring my options, I began selling Windings to its employees through an ESOP. I sold 13% at a time until the ESOP reached majority ownership, and then I sold two 15% tranches. At this point, I wanted to sell the rest of the company in a transaction that was financed with a local bank.*
>
> *When I acquired Windings in 1983, it was a $700,000-per-year business. By the time I sold my last portion to the ESOP, it was a $25 million business and financially strong such that the local bank that financed the final transaction didn't even ask my wife and me to cosign the loan! And it's only grown stronger since then, doubling in share value in the time since I left in 2008.*
>
> *Most of all, I'm proud to say that our company is still a thriving and important part of the community, one that is owned by all the people who continue to make it great.*

In 1974, Congress agreed to Kelso's ideas about the value of employee ownership and created a series of tax incentives for what was labelled an employee stock ownership plan (ESOP), incorporating them in a massive reform of retirement law known as ERISA (the

Employee Retirement Income Security Act of 1974). Congress basically made a deal with employers: share ownership with employees and in return get a tax deduction for doing so. In addition, ESOPs would be allowed to borrow money to buy company stock, something no other benefit plan could do. That loan would be repaid out of tax-deductible corporate contributions, not employee purchases. Over the years, Congress sweetened that basic deal with a variety of additional tax incentives, including allowing certain sellers to ESOPs to defer capital gains tax on the sale of their stock, letting companies deduct dividends paid on ESOP shares if certain rules were met, and, ultimately, excluding from federal corporate income tax the ESOP's percentage of ownership in an S corporation, making a 100% ESOP-owned S corporation non-taxable. In return for all this, companies had to make sure the plans were run in a way that truly benefited employees on a broad and equitable basis.

That basic deal has led today to roughly 6,600 ESOPs and ESOP-like plans, covering more than 14 million participants. Of these, only about 8% are in publicly traded companies; the rest are in closely held companies. The NCEO estimates the median percentage ownership for ESOPs in public companies is about 1% to 10%. Most public companies maintain an ESOP along with other benefit plans. The NCEO estimates that the median ownership percentage for private companies is closer to 50%, and probably a third are 100% ESOP-owned. While the typical company has 20 to 500 employees, employees own a majority of the stock of such companies as Publix Super Markets (200,000 employees), Houchens Industries (18,000 employees), and WinCo (18,000 employees). About three-quarters of ESOPs in private companies are used to buy out an owner; the rest are typically used simply as employee benefit plans, sometimes in conjunction with borrowing money for capital acquisition.

Overall, providing generous tax incentives for ESOPs has been a good policy. Employees in ESOP companies have somewhat higher wages than comparable employees in comparable non-ESOP companies, but they also have about three times the company-related retirement assets. ESOP companies grow about 2% to 3% per year faster than would have been expected without an ESOP. Those that combine an ESOP with an "ownership culture" (one that emphasizes open-book management and high employee involvement in work-level decisions) grow 6% to 11% per year faster. Of course, these are averages. Some companies do incredibly well; others (such as Enron and United Airlines) are disasters.

> ### The Mud Bay ESOP
> Mud Bay is a chain of pet stores in the Northwest that set up an ESOP in 2015, the same year it was named retailer of the year by *Pet Business* magazine. Led by Lars, Marissa, and Elsa Wulff, the company has grown 15% per year for several years by creating an exceptional high-involvement culture, with employees involved in all aspects of store operations and decisions. Employees are paid well and have exceptional benefits, and return the favor with enthusiasm, loyalty, and expertise. The Wulffs don't have any current plans to give up majority family ownership, but they will fund the ESOP each year out of company profits to build a substantial ownership stake for employees. Co-CEO Lars Wulff told *Pet Business* in 2015 that "We believe that being an owner-operator has helped make our work for Mud Bay fulfilling, and we want all of Mud Bay's staff to have the same experience. Sharing ownership with staff just seems fair—like the right thing to do."

The ESOP Proposition

As noted above, in creating an ESOP, a company sets up an employee benefit trust, which it funds by contributing cash to buy company stock, contributing shares directly, or having the trust borrow money to buy stock, with the company making contributions to the plan to enable it to repay the loan. Generally, at least all full-time employees with a year or more of service are in the plan. To assure that these rules are met, the board appoints a trustee to act as the plan fiduciary. Some ESOP company boards appoint an ESOP fiduciary committee, usually made up of insiders but occasionally with outsiders as well, to make decisions for the plan and instruct the formal trustee how to act. The trustee can be anyone, although larger companies tend to appoint outside trust institutions, while smaller companies typically appoint managers or create ESOP trust committees. ESOPs are designed to invest primarily in the stock of the employer and can buy treasury shares, newly issued shares, or shares from exiting owners.

There is one very important point that is widely misunderstood: employees almost never contribute to the plan; instead, contributions are funded by the company as a benefit, and shares are allocated to employee accounts on a nondiscriminatory basis, much as in a profit-sharing plan. It's worth repeating that: *as a rule, employees do not buy shares in an ESOP.* Over the years, we have found that many people considering an ESOP have a difficult time understanding how that can be. The answer is simple: the company funds the plan instead.

An ESOP can be used for many purposes, including the following:

- *To buy the shares of a departing owner of a closely held company.* This is the most common application. In C corporations, owners can defer tax on the gains they have made from the sale to an ESOP if the ESOP holds 30% or more of the company's stock and certain other requirements are met. Moreover, the purchase can be made in pretax corporate dollars, whether the company is C or S.
- *To divest or acquire subsidiaries, buy back shares from the market, or restructure existing benefit plans by replacing current benefit contributions with a leveraged ESOP.*
- *To buy newly issued shares in the company, with the borrowed funds being used to buy new productive capital.* The company

can, in effect, finance growth or acquisitions in pretax dollars while these same dollars create an employee benefit plan.

- *To simply be an employee benefit plan for companies that want to share ownership broadly.* In public companies especially, an ESOP contribution is often used as part or all of a match to employee deferrals to a 401(k) plan.

These benefits come in return for operating the plan under ERISA guidelines. Passed in 1974 in the wake of pension scandals, the law was broadly drafted to cover a variety of employee benefit plans, including health insurance, pension plans, profit-sharing plans, ESOPs, retirement savings plans, cafeteria plans, and other benefits meant to provide financial security to a broad group of employees. The basic idea is straightforward: the government provides employees and employers with tax breaks if their plans provide benefits on a nondiscriminatory basis across the work force. To do that, ERISA relies on several key concepts:

- *Operate the plan for the "exclusive benefit of plan participants."* Despite how it sounds, a plan can benefit companies and other people as well, but when there is a conflict of interest, the interests of participants should prevail.

- *Govern the plan with an "eye single" to the interests of participants.* The plan trustee is required by law to make sure the plan is operated primarily for the benefit of the people in it, not for the company or its owners. In an ESOP, this means, among other things, not overpaying for company stock.

- *Make prudent investment decisions for the plan.* Any funds in ERISA plans used for retirement should be invested in a way that a sensible, careful investor would invest them. Excess risk is discouraged, but so is parking all the money in a passbook savings account. There is a special exception for ESOPs, however. Here, ERISA not only permits but requires plans to be primarily invested in company stock, unless it is clear that the investment is in imminent danger of failing.

- *Broadly include those who work for the company and meet minimal requirements.* Generally, this means at a minimum all employees who have worked for at least 1,000 hours in a year must become eligible in the following year. There are some exceptions, however, such as employees covered by a bargaining agreement or employees in a separate line of business.[1]
- *Allocate benefits fairly.* Benefits can be allocated based on relative pay or a more level formula, but pay over $285,000 (as of 2020; this amount is indexed for inflation) does not count.
- *Make benefits subject to vesting.* Most retirement plans allow companies to require that employees stay a certain amount of time before they earn any benefits contributed by the company.
- *Have a process for employees to contest decisions.* ERISA spells out a variety of specific procedures by which employees can argue that they were improperly denied benefits. The first level is to try to resolve the matter within the company. The second is to ask the government to step in (usually the U.S. Department of Labor [DOL], although the DOL's resources for this are limited). The third is to sue in federal courts.
- *Preserve the benefit in a trust for long-term wealth building.* All retirement plans governed by ERISA provide the employee with special tax benefits. Unlike other ownership arrangements we discuss in this book, ownership through an ESOP is not taxed when the employee is vested in the benefit, but rather when it is received (which normally is some time much later, such as after the employee leaves the company). But employees usually have only a limited ability to take money out of the plan while still

---

1. There are also provisions that allow a company to exclude up to 30% of its non-highly compensated employees who otherwise meet the requirements, but it is extremely rare and usually impractical for ESOP companies to use this exception.

working (mostly in 401(k) plans through loans) and face a tax penalty if they don't put the money in an IRA or other retirement account when they actually get it after leaving the company.

In short, if you want the benefits of one of these plans, you have to meet a number of rules. You cannot pick and choose who you want to allow to be in the plan, nor can you base their awards on assessments of merit or adopt other discretionary approaches. If you can live with that, however, these plans are greatly more financially advantageous, to the company and the employee, than other approaches.

Funding

The most sophisticated use of an ESOP is to borrow money. The company borrows money from a lender and reloans it to the ESOP; the ESOP then uses the money to buy shares. The company makes tax-deductible contributions to the trust to enable it to repay the loan. This is called a "leveraged" ESOP. The company can also use dividends paid on shares (in C corporations) or distributions of earnings (in S corporations) to repay the loan; these dividends are deductible if the company is a C corporation (in 100% ESOP-owned S corporations, there is no tax anyway, so deductions are not an issue). In effect, the parallel loan structure allows the company to borrow money to acquire stock and, by funneling the loan through the ESOP, deduct both principal and interest. The company can use proceeds from the loan for any legitimate business purpose. Sellers to an ESOP can also be lenders. The stock is put into a "suspense account," from where it is released to employee accounts as the loan is repaid.

The ESOP can also be funded directly by discretionary corporate contributions of cash that are used to buy existing shares or simply by the contribution of shares. These contributions to an ESOP are tax-deductible, generally up to 25% of the total eligible payroll of plan participants, although there is a limit on the deductibility of interest of 30% of EBITDA as of 2018, and 30% of EBIT in 2022 and beyond for businesses with more than $25 million in gross receipts.

How Shares Get to Employees

If the company contributes shares or cash to buy shares, these contributions are immediately allocated to employee accounts in the plan. In a leveraged ESOP, the acquired shares are placed in a suspense account. As the loan is repaid, a percentage of the total shares acquired is released to employee accounts in an amount equal to either the principal paid that year or the percentage of total principal plus interest due that is paid that year. The amount *contributed* to repay the principal on the loan is what counts for determining whether the company is within the limits for contributions allowed each year and for the purpose of calculating the tax deduction. The *value* of the shares released, however, is the amount used on the corporate income statement, where it counts as a compensation cost. From the employees' perspective, it is this value of shares released that will also matter to them because this is the amount they will see added to their accounts.

Companies can also use dividends or (in S corporations) earnings distributions to pay for leveraged shares. In that case, the dividends paid on the shares allocated to employee accounts must release shares to employee accounts at least equal in value to the dividends, and are allocated based on relative share balances. Shares that have not yet been paid for are released to employee accounts based on how much of the remaining value of the shares is repaid and can be allocated based either on the employees' current relative account balances or on the same formula used for releasing shares paid for by company contributions.

Once the shares are in the plan, the rules for ESOPs are similar to the rules for other tax-qualified ERISA plans in terms of who is a plan participant, how allocations are made, vesting, and distribution, but several special considerations apply.

At least all employees over age 21 who work for more than 1,000 hours in a plan year must be included in the next plan year (or earlier) unless they are covered by a collective bargaining unit (and the ESOP issue is negotiated in good faith) or are in a separate line of business with at least 50 employees not covered by the ESOP, or fall into one of several limited anti-discrimination exemptions. Companies can always have more liberal rules for participation.

An alternative approach provides three tests for coverage. To use this approach, a company applies percentage tests to at least a minimum employee group. This group must include all employees 21 or older who have completed at least 1,000 hours of service in a plan year, but it can exclude nonresident aliens, employees in a separate line of business with 50 or more employees, and employees covered by a collective bargaining agreement. After these exceptions have been taken, the tests can be met if:

1. At least 70% of non-highly compensated employees are covered, or
2. The percentage of non-highly compensated employees who are covered is at least 70% of the percentage of highly compensated employees covered, or
3. There is a classification system that does not discriminate in favor of highly compensated employees, and the average benefit percentage (generally, the percentage of compensation contributed to the plan) for the covered non-highly compensated group is at least 70% of that contributed to the covered highly compensated group.

Few ESOPs, however, use these alternative tests, both because they want to create a culture of ownership that is inclusive and because how much can be contributed to a plan overall is limited by the payroll of employees in the plan (meaning that a company wishing to maximize the amount the ESOP can buy will want to maximize plan participation).

Plans have one or more "entry dates" for employees once they become participants. An employee who has satisfied the plan's minimum age and service requirements must begin participation in the plan not later than the first of (1) the first day of the plan year beginning after the date on which the requirements were met or (2) the date six months after the date on which the requirements are met. Participation can begin at an earlier date, however. Many plans, for example, have entry dates every six months or every year, and employees become participants at the first entry date after requirements are met.

Shares are usually allocated to individual employee accounts based on relative eligible compensation. Some companies use an alternative formula, generally providing some points for relative pay and some for tenure or, less often, a per-capita allocation. Generally, all W-2 compensation is counted, but there is leeway to define compensation differently, such as by excluding bonuses, provided that it does not favor more highly compensated individuals; on a more level formula, such as per capita, by seniority, or by placing a cap on pay that can be considered; or some combination of the two, such as one point for seniority and one for relative pay. If relative eligible pay is not used, plans must be tested annually to determine whether any highly compensated individual, generally defined as someone belonging to either the top 20% by payroll in the company or those making more than $130,000 per year (as of 2020), is receiving more than what the relative pay formula would indicate. In that case, the excess must be returned to the plan and reallocated to other participants. Finally, ESOP allocations can be used as a match to employee deferrals to a 401(k) plan, in which case all or part of the allocation may be determined by how much the employee defers. This approach requires complex anti-discrimination testing for both plans. Relatively few ESOPs use this approach.

Eligible compensation includes the pay of only those employees actually participating in the plan. As noted earlier, it excludes pay over $285,000 (as of 2020). It also excludes the pay of sellers to an ESOP who take advantage of the ability to defer tax on the gains from the sale proceeds, as well as their immediate relatives, more-than-25% owners, and certain relatives of the more-than-25% owners.

The allocated shares are subject to vesting. If the plan provides for vesting all at once, called cliff vesting, employees must be 100% vested after three years of service; if vesting is gradual, it must not be slower than 20% after two years and 20% more per year until 100% is reached after six years. Plans can vest faster than these schedules. Companies do not have to provide credit for years of service before the ESOP, but many companies do. Some companies give a year of credit for every year of prior service; some give a year for every x number of years.

When employees reach age 55 and have 10 years of participation in the plan, the company must in the next five years either give them the option of diversifying 25% of company stock in their account balances among at least three other investment alternatives or simply pay the amount out to the employees. During the sixth year, employees can have a cumulative total of 50% diversified or distributed to them.

When employees retire, die, or become disabled, the company must distribute their vested shares to them not later than the last day of the plan year following the year of their departure. For employees leaving before reaching retirement age, distribution must begin not later than the last day of the sixth plan year following their year of separation from service. Payments can be in substantially equal installments out of the trust over five years, or they can be made in a lump sum. With the installment method, a company normally pays out a portion of the stock from the trust each year.

Closely held companies and some thinly traded public companies must repurchase the shares from departing employees at their fair market value, as determined by an independent appraiser. This so-called "put option" can be exercised by the employee in one of two 60-day periods, one starting when the employee receives the distribution and the second period one year after that. The employee can choose which one to use. This obligation should be considered at the outset of the ESOP and be factored into the company's ability to repay the loan.

This repurchase obligation should be assessed on a periodic basis. There are a variety of ways to fund the obligation, including making cash contributions to the ESOP to enable it to buy back the shares, building a cash reserve, using insurance proceeds, releveraging the ESOP, and other techniques. The impact of the obligation on valuation should be calculated. Normally, the obligation will reduce future share prices somewhat if share prices are growing, making future repurchases more manageable.

> ### Voices from ESOP Companies
>
> "Each person has a stake in the company—you can see it, you can feel it. Not only am I happier at work, but I now have a financial plan for my future (in my ESOP) that I didn't have before (and never expected to have). I wish every company in the U.S. were an ESOP company. But mostly, I wish I had found Web 20 years sooner."
> —Rosanne Wheeler-Flint, customer care specialist, Web Industries
>
> "The ESOP form of ownership is the best way that I have seen for middle-class Americans to save for a secure retirement since the disappearance of the pension system. For the company, the benefits in recruiting and employee retention are substantial."
> —Jay Bondurant, financial analyst, King Arthur Flour

Limitations on Contributions

Congress was generous in providing tax benefits for ESOPs, but there are limits. Generally, companies can contribute and deduct an amount equal to up to 25% of the total eligible payroll of plan participants, whether contributed in the form of cash or stock or in payments to fund the repayment of an ESOP loan. Eligible pay is essentially all the pay (including employee deferrals into benefit plans) of people actually in the plan up to $285,000 per participant (as of 2020; like the other dollar limits described here for defined contribution plans, this is indexed annually for inflation).

In C corporations, there are separate 25% deductibility limits for (1) contributions to pay principal on an ESOP loan (interest is deductible as it always is on a loan) and (2) additional contributions to the ESOP or to other defined contribution plans, provided they are not used to repay interest or principal on the ESOP loan. A company with a leveraged ESOP and a profit-sharing plan, for example, has a 50% total deductibility limit (up to 25% for a leveraged ESOP plus up to 25% for other defined contributions not related to the loan). However, in S corporations, company contributions to a leveraged or non-leveraged ESOP and other defined contribution plans all fall under a single 25%-of-eligible-pay calculation. Interest payments on the ESOP loan are deductible as interest, but the company cannot deduct more than 25% of eligible pay to cover both the interest and principal payments.

On top of this, in C corporations, "reasonable" dividends paid on shares acquired by the ESOP can be used to repay an ESOP loan, and these are not included in the 25%-of-pay calculations. S corporations can use distributions on earnings to help repay the loan, although these are not deductible as they are in C corporations (but they are also not taxable to the ESOP). In a leveraged ESOP in a C corporation, if employees leave the company before they have a fully vested right to their shares, their forfeitures, which are allocated to everyone else, are not counted in the percentage limitations. They are counted in an S corporation ESOP, however.

There are a number of limitations to these provisions, however. First, no one ESOP participant can get a contribution of more than 100% of pay in any year from the principal payments on the loan or the direct ESOP contributions made that year that are attributable to that employee, or more than $57,000 (as of 2020), whichever is less. In figuring payroll, pay over $285,000 per year (as of 2020) does not count toward total contribution limits. Second, if there are other qualified benefit plans, these must be taken into account when assessing this limit. This means that employee deferrals into 401(k) plans, as well as other employer contributions to 401(k) plans, stock bonus, or profit-sharing plans, are added to the ESOP contribution and cannot exceed 100% of pay or $57,000 (as of 2020) in any year.

Third, the interest on an ESOP loan repayment in a C corporation is excludable from the 25%-of-pay individual limit only if not more than one-third of the benefits are allocated to "highly compensated employees," as defined by Internal Revenue Code Section 414(q). If the one-third rule is not met, forfeitures are also counted in determining how much an employee is getting each year.

Voting

In private companies, employees must be able to direct the trustee as to the voting of shares *allocated* to their accounts on several key issues, including closing, sale, liquidation, recapitalization, and other issues having to do with the basic structure of the company. They do not, however, have to be able to vote for the board of directors or on other typical corporate governance issues, although companies can voluntarily provide these rights. Instead, the plan trustee votes the shares. An independent trustee will use its own judgment but usually look to the board for guidance on issues such as board elections. Directed trustees will follow the instructions of the board or an ESOP committee—a group of individuals, usually (but not always) insiders, who take on a fiduciary role in directing the trustee as to how to vote. In public companies, employees must be able to vote on all issues.

What these rules mean is that governance is not really an issue for ESOP companies unless they want it to be. If companies want employees to have only the most limited role in corporate governance, they can; if they want to go beyond this, they can as well. In practice, companies that do provide employees with a substantial governance role find that it does not result in dramatic changes in the way the company is run.

Finally, in private companies and some thinly traded public companies, all ESOP transactions must be based on a current appraisal by an independent, outside valuation expert.

Tax Benefits to the Selling Shareholder

One of the major benefits of an ESOP for closely held C corporations is found in Section 1042 of the Internal Revenue Code. Under it, a seller to an ESOP may be able to qualify for a deferral of taxation on the gain made from the sale. Several requirements apply, the most significant of which are:

1. The seller must have held the stock for three years before the sale.
2. The stock must not have been acquired through stock options or other employee benefit plans.
3. The ESOP must own 30% or more of the value of the company's shares and must continue to hold this amount for three years unless the company is sold. Shares the company repurchases from departing employees do not count. Stock sold in a transaction that brings the ESOP to 30% of the total shares qualifies for the deferral treatment.
4. Shares qualifying for the deferral cannot be allocated to the accounts of the selling shareholder(s); to lineal descendants, brothers or sisters, spouses, or parents of the selling shareholder(s); or to any more-than-25% shareholders.

If these rules are met, the seller (or sellers) can take the proceeds from the sale and reinvest them in "qualified replacement property" during the period running from 3 months before to 12 months after the sale and defer any capital gains tax until these new investments are sold. Qualified replacement property essentially means stocks, bonds, warrants, or debentures of domestic corporations receiving not more than 25% of their income from passive investment. Mutual funds and real estate trusts do not qualify. If the replacement securities are held until death, they are subject to a step-up in basis at that time, so capital gains taxes would never be paid.

With the passage of the tax reform legislation popularly known as the Tax Cuts and Jobs Act of 2017 (the "2017 Act"), selling to an ESOP and deferring taxes under Section 1042 has become more appealing, especially to owners in high-tax states, because there is now a cap of $10,000 on the amount of state and local income taxes that can be deducted from gross income. If, for example, an owner in California, where the top marginal tax rate is 13.3%, sells $5 million in stock to a non-ESOP buyer, the seller would pay well over half a million dollars in California taxes. Before the 2017 Act, the California taxes would have been deducted from the seller's federal gross income, but the 2017 Act limits that deduction to $10,000. The result could be a significant additional tax benefit to selling to an ESOP and not declaring any of the proceeds as nondeductible state income. This difference will be meaningful only in states with higher tax rates on capital gains, of course, and is unlikely to be a deciding issue, but it does add to the attractiveness of using the Section 1042 deferral.

Very often, lenders ask for replacement securities as part or all of the collateral for an ESOP loan. This strategy may be beneficial to sellers selling only part of their holdings because it frees the corporation to use its assets for other borrowing and could enhance the future value of the company.

As with all transactions in closely held ESOP companies, the price the ESOP pays for the shares cannot be more than fair market value as assessed by an independent appraiser. The price is what a financial buyer would pay—someone who would operate the company as a stand-alone entity, not as part of another enterprise as a synergistic buyer might. That means an ESOP may not be able to meet the price of some synergistic buyers, although it does offer better tax benefits on the sale.

Corporate Tax Benefits

As noted above, companies can use ESOPs to borrow money and repay the loan entirely in pretax dollars. In addition, companies can take a tax deduction for reasonable dividends that are used to repay a loan, that are passed through directly to employees, or that employees voluntarily reinvest in company stock. Contributions not used to repay an ESOP loan are tax-deductible as well, even if made in the form of treasury shares or new shares. However, the 2017 Act limits net interest deductions for businesses to 30% of EBITDA (earnings before interest, taxes, depreciation, and amortization) for four years, at which point the limit decreases to 30% of EBIT in 2022. A company with a new leveraged ESOP that borrows an amount that is large relative to its EBITDA may find that its deductible expenses will be lower and, therefore, that its taxable income may be higher under the new rules. This change will not affect 100% ESOP-owned S corporations because they do not pay tax. As we go to press, many questions remain on the impact of this change.

ESOPs in S Corporations

ESOPs can own stock in S corporations. While these ESOPs operate under most of the same rules as they do in C corporations, there are important differences. As noted above, interest payments on S corporation ESOP loans count toward the contribution limits (they normally do not in C companies). Dividends (i.e., S corporation "distributions") paid on ESOP shares are also not deductible. Most important, sellers to an ESOP in an S corporation do not qualify for the tax-deferred Section 1042 rollover treatment.

On the other hand, the ESOP is unique among S corporation owners in that it does not have to pay federal income tax on any profits attributable to it (state rules vary). This can make an ESOP very attractive in some cases. It also makes converting to S corporation status very appealing when a C corporation's ESOP owns a high percentage of the company's stock.

For S corporation owners who want to use an ESOP to provide a market for their shares, generally it will make sense to convert to C status before setting up an ESOP. Where selling shares is not a priority, or where the seller either does not have substantial capital gains taxes due on the sale or has other reasons to retain S corporation status, an S corporation ESOP can provide significant tax benefits. However, keep in mind that any distributions paid to owners must be paid pro-rata to the ESOP. The ESOP can use these distributions to purchase additional shares, to build up cash for future repurchases of employee shares, or just to add to employee accounts.

While the S corporation rules make an ESOP very attractive, legislation passed in 2001 made it clear that companies may not create an ESOP primarily to benefit a few people. For instance, some accountants were promoting plans in which a company would set up an S corporation management company owned by just a few people that would manage a large C corporation. The C corporation's profits would flow through the S corporation's ESOP and thus not be taxed.

The rules Congress enacted are complicated, but they boil down to two essential points. First, people who own 10% or more of the "deemed-owned" shares, or who own 20% or more counting their family members, are considered "disqualified" persons. "Deemed-owned shares" are defined to include what is allocated in the ESOP, a pro-rata share of unallocated shares in the trust, and any synthetic equity rights, such as phantom stock, stock options, stock appreciation rights, warrants, and certain kinds of deferred compensation the IRS considers equity-rights equivalents. Second, if these disqualified people together own 50% or more of the company's equity (counting their synthetic equity), then there will be devastating tax penalties. Congress also directed the IRS to apply this onerous tax treatment to any plan it deems to be substantially for the purpose of evading taxes rather than providing employee benefits.

Comparing ESOPs to Other Business Transition Strategies

Many business owners choose to do ESOPs primarily because of personal and philosophical reasons and do not seriously consider other strategies for liquidity. But for those who consider the ESOP one option among others, it is worthwhile comparing some essential aspects of an ESOP versus a sale to a third party. Table 1-1 lays out key considerations.

ESOPs compare especially favorably to redemptions or sales to insiders. Redemptions are done in after-tax dollars, meaning a company will have to generate about 60% more revenue to buy stock than if the money were pretax, as in an ESOP. Similarly, insiders have to use after-tax money to buy shares.

Financial Issues for Employees

When an employee receives a distribution from the plan, it is taxable unless rolled over into an IRA or other qualified account. Otherwise, the amounts contributed by the employer are taxable as ordinary income, while any appreciation on the shares is taxable as capital gains. In addition, if the employee receives the distribution before normal retirement age and does not roll over the funds, a 10% excise tax is added.

While the stock is in the plan, however, it is not taxable to employees. It is rare, moreover, for employees to give up wages to participate in an ESOP or to purchase stock directly through a plan (this raises difficult securities law issues for closely held firms). Most ESOPs either are in addition to existing benefit plans or replace other defined contribution plans, usually at a higher contribution level.

Accounting

In nonleveraged plans, the contribution to the ESOP shows up directly as a compensation cost. In leveraged plans, the principal pay-

Table 1-1. Sale to an ESOP vs. a third party

	ESOPs	Third party
Document requirements	ESOP plans and trustee agreements must be created, along with lender agreements and sale terms	Detailed selling memorandum, non-compete agreements, financing arrangements, escrow accounts, and other contractual matters
Implementation costs	Most initial ESOP transaction costs range between $75,000 and $125,000, but some transactions can be more expensive, depending on complexity and size	Legal and advisory costs may be somewhat lower, but many sales involve broker fees paid as a percentage of the transaction
Implementation time	Generally 6–12 months	Generally 6–12 months
Contingencies	ESOPs rarely involve contingencies on the price paid	Most sales involve some contingencies, such as earnouts, financing, or escrow
Valuation	Based on a third-party appraisal based on what a financial buyer would pay	Based on a negotiation; a minority of companies may attract a synergistic price, although often with contingencies
Sale of minority interest	Commonly done in ESOPs	Very difficult to do in non-ESOP transactions unless the company has substantial growth prospects and liquidity options in the near term
Taxes	Seller can defer taxation in qualifying ESOP sales	Seller pays capital gains taxes (in an asset sale, capital gains taxes would be paid both on asset and stock appreciation in C corporations)

ments and dividend payments on unallocated shares that are used to repay a loan show up as a compensation charge as well; dividends on allocated shares show up as a charge to retained earnings. The debt of the ESOP shows up as corporate debt, with an offsetting contra equity account that is reduced as the loan is repaid.

Ownership, Corporate Culture, and Corporate Performance

Many executives believe that if they share ownership and explain it well enough to people, then employees will perform better. It is not that simple, however. Employee ownership can improve corporate performance significantly, but only when combined with what we call an "ownership culture." Ownership culture companies share financial information with employees on a regular basis and get employees involved in work-level decisions. They seek out not just more employee effort to do the same things better, but more employee ideas to do things better—or do new things entirely.

On the financial level, these companies typically share some version of the income statement and balance sheet on a periodic basis. More important, they break numbers down into usable small pieces that measure key performance indicators for the company and for employee groups, such as quality control, output, backlog, customer satisfaction, on-time delivery, etc. These numbers provide employees with targets they can easily grasp and work to meet or exceed. The best companies get employees involved in generating these numbers as well.

Employees also have regular opportunities for input through work teams, quality circles, ad hoc committees, suggestion systems, informal and formal meetings with managers, and other opportunities. Management does not just pay lip service to the idea of empowering employees to make more decisions; it really does it. Ownership culture companies find that, over time, employee ideas get better and better, and that more of the work force becomes engaged in finding ways to help the company make money.

Conclusion

ESOPs are hard work. They take time to understand and implement; it takes even more time and effort to create a true ownership culture.

But go to an ESOP meeting and you will meet company leaders who are not just glad they did it, but absolutely evangelical. Not only are they succeeding and enjoying the tax benefits of ESOPs, but they are also just flat-out having more fun. ESOPs are not right for everyone, but if you are willing to make this effort, they are well worth considering.

Chapter 2

Selling to an ESOP in a Closely Held Company
Scott Rodrick

As chapter 1 states, the most popular use of an ESOP is to buy the shares of a departing owner in a closely held company. This chapter goes into more detail on why this happens and discusses the rules for a major tax incentive for selling owners in C corporations, the tax-deferred "rollover" of funds from an ESOP sale, plus some major considerations that go into deciding whether to sell to an ESOP and whether to elect the tax-deferred "rollover."

Why a Sale to an ESOP Often Makes Sense

An ESOP is not for everyone, but in many cases, it is the best way for someone to sell shares in a closely held company they own. As a tax-exempt employee benefit plan trust, the ESOP offers flexible, tax-advantaged treatment and does not have the restrictions, covenants, employment consequences, and other problems that can arise with an outside buyer.

The ESOP Creates a Market for the Shares in Any Amount

After years of building their companies, many small business owners find themselves at an impasse when the time comes to leave. Sometimes a family member or members may be willing and able to take over, but even then, the owner may wish to sell part or all of his or her ownership interest, and it may not be practical for personal or financial reasons for family members to buy out the owner. Company managers or other employees may be interested in buying shares, but buying the entire company may be financially unfeasible. Moving beyond the sphere of family members and employees, the owner may seek an outside buyer, but that too can be difficult (and expensive if a business broker is used).

If the would-be seller owns a minority interest in the company, or owns more but wants to sell only a part of the company, outside buyers may not be interested. Often, there are multiple owners of a closely held company, and at any given time, only a few may be interested in selling. And even if several people want to sell, their interests may still amount to a small percentage. The remaining owners may not want to deal with the proposed new owners.

An ESOP solves these dilemmas by creating a market for the shares. It can buy any percentage of the company; thus, an owner or owners can sell anything from a small percentage to all of the company to the ESOP.

Owners Can Sell Gradually to the ESOP While Staying with the Business

A potential buyer, especially an outside one, often will want to buy an owner's interest all at once. In contrast, an ESOP is flexible and, in addition to being able to buy any percentage of the shares (as noted above), can buy shares gradually so the owner can slowly exit his or her investment.

If the selling owner is the CEO or holds another major executive position at the company, an outside buyer often will wish to replace him or her with someone else (perhaps retaining the owner as a consultant for some period). If the ESOP is the buyer, however, there is no need for the selling owner to leave the company unless he or she desires to.

An ESOP Preserves the Stability of the Company

Sometimes people worry that since rank-and-file employees become beneficial owners through the ESOP trust, the company will be turned upside down and "the inmates will run the asylum." The truth is actually the opposite. If someone sells a company to an outsider, especially one that merely wants the company for its assets or to gain a strategic advantage over a competitor, the seller may wake up one day to find that all the managers have been fired (they are often the first people to be discarded or replaced), that beloved rank-and-file employees have been fired, or even that the company has been shut down after being stripped of its assets. With an ESOP, in contrast, the company stays the same; the only difference is that the stock now happens to be held by an employee trust (the ESOP trust) instead of the former owners. The ESOP trustee, selected by the company's board, in turn votes for the board in the trustee's capacity as a shareholder, unless the company chooses to pass the vote through to the ESOP participants.[1]

Employees Will Gain Ownership and Motivation

From the seller's point of view, an ESOP provides an excellent market for company shares. Something else to consider is that employ-

---

1. In that case, the trustee would still vote the shares (because the ESOP trust is the shareholder), but would do so as instructed by the ESOP participants. The company would do this by having the ESOP plan document drafted to provide for such voting rights.

ees will gain a valuable benefit (i.e., stock in their ESOP accounts). Furthermore, as discussed elsewhere in this book, the combination of employee ownership through an ESOP and a management style that recognizes that ownership can result in a more motivated workforce and thus a more profitable company.

An ESOP Is Cost-Effective for the Owner and Company

If a business broker is used to sell the company to an outside buyer, a large fee may be charged. Aside from this, the selling owner will have to pay what may be an enormous tax bill if it is a cash transaction. It is possible to structure a company sale as a tax-free reorganization in which another company acquires the seller's company in exchange for stock. Again, this raises the issue of having to sell most or all of the company, which may not be desirable or even possible, given other owners or a desire to sell only a part of the company. And, depending on the transaction structure, the company may cease to exist, at least in its old form. Finally, the owner ends up with an undiversified investment in somebody else's company and has two choices: either keep that stock and pray that it does not lose value as the years go by and that it can be sold someday, or sell the stock now and pay taxes.

Alternatively, the owner may seek a sale by corporate redemption, but this is not tax-efficient for anyone because the owner pays taxes and the company receives no tax deduction.

In contrast, an ESOP offers considerable tax advantages. The company's contributions to pay for the buyout are tax-deductible. This means, for example, that a $3 million sale to the ESOP does not require the company to first earn at least $4 million or so, pay taxes, and then take the $3 million remaining to fund the buyout. With an ESOP, the funds used to buy out an owner ($3 million in this example) are pretax.

In a C corporation, the owner can indefinitely defer taxation on the proceeds of the transaction by reinvesting them in securities of

U.S. companies and electing the Section 1042 tax deferral (discussed below). In an S corporation, the Section 1042 tax deferral is not available. However, there is a separate tax advantage: there will be no federal tax (and, depending on the state, often no state tax) on corporate income attributable to the ESOP, which means that the company will not need to pay distributions to fund tax bills if the ESOP owns all of the company.

The Section 1042 Tax-Deferred Rollover

For countless business owners over the years, one of the main reasons for selling to an ESOP has been the ability to indefinitely postpone taxation on the gains by electing tax-deferred "rollover" treatment under Section 1042 of the Internal Revenue Code (the "Code"). In a nutshell, when an owner in a closely held C corporation sells to an ESOP that owns 30% or more of the company (including the amount the ESOP holds after the transaction), the seller can defer taxation indefinitely by "rolling over" the sales proceeds into stocks and bonds of U.S. companies (the "Section 1042 rollover," also referred to here by such terms as "the Section 1042 tax deferral" or "Section 1042 treatment"). Furthermore, if the selling owner holds the newly bought stocks or bonds until death, there will be a step-up in basis, and his or her heirs will pay no capital gains tax. Section 1042 treatment does not arise automatically; the selling owner must formally elect the tax deferral and file required paperwork, as described below.

For some years, Section 1042 has not been as important as it once was in the ESOP community. For example, capital gains rates are not as high as they once were. However, the Section 1042 rollover remains an important consideration, and it is the only ESOP tax incentive that is given to the selling owner. Moreover, with the passage of the Tax Cuts and Jobs Act in 2017, the state and local tax deduction at the federal level was capped at $10,000 (including property taxes) for tax years beginning in 2018, meaning that Section 1042 transactions may now be considerably more attractive to business owners in high-tax states. For example, a seller receiving several million dollars from an ESOP transaction and paying several hundred thousand dollars in state-level taxes formerly could deduct those state taxes from income for federal tax purposes. Now the seller is limited to a $10,000 deduction (which itself might be used up by property taxes), meaning that the seller's federal taxable income in this example would increase by several hundred thousand dollars.

There are many requirements for the Section 1042 tax deferral, so they will be discussed one by one.

The Company Must Be a Closely Held C Corporation

Section 1042 applies only to a sale to an ESOP in a C corporation. An S corporation can allow selling owners to elect the Section 1042 tax deferral by converting to C status before the ESOP transaction. If it does this, however, it must wait at least five years before re-electing S status.

The company must be closely held as well: for at least one year before and after the sale, the company (and each corporation belonging to a controlled group of corporations with the company) must have no stock that is tradable on "an established securities market."

The ESOP Must Own 30% or More of the Company After the Sale

The ESOP need not hold any shares before the sale, and the sale itself need not be of any particular amount, but after the sale, the ESOP must own 30% or more of either each class of outstanding stock or the total value of all of the company's outstanding stock (excluding in each case nonvoting, nonconvertible preferred stock).[2]

---

2. Thus, an ESOP could be formed, holding no stock at first, and then a 30% sale made, which would allow the selling owner to elect the tax deferral on all of the sale proceeds. Alternatively, an ESOP could have been established some years ago and hold 29% of the company. The owner could now sell 1%,

Two or more sellers may aggregate their sales to meet the "30% after the sale" requirement if the sales are part of a single, integrated transaction that they prearrange. For example, if owner X and owner Y each sell 15% of the company in such an integrated transaction, the IRS will not say, "The ESOP held only 15% after owner X sold, so X cannot elect Section 1042 treatment"; rather, it will look at the entire transaction, in which the ESOP ended up with 30%.

In determining what constitutes 30% ownership, Section 1042(b)(2) applies Code Section 318(a)(4), which provides that "[i]f any person has an option to acquire stock, such stock shall be considered as owned by such person." For example, if the ESOP would otherwise own 30% of the company after the transaction but someone has an option (or equivalent security such as a warrant) to buy shares in an amount that would dilute the ESOP's ownership under 30%, the transaction will fail the 30% test.

The Seller Must Be an Individual or One of Certain Other Entities

To elect the Section 1042 tax deferral, a seller must be an individual, a partnership, a (taxable) trust, an estate, or a limited liability company (LLC). The seller cannot be a C nor (apparently) an S corporation. If the seller is a partnership or LLC, the partnership or LLC makes the 1042 election, not individual partners or members.

The Stock Must Have Been Held for Three Years and Cannot Be from a Qualified Stock Plan

Generally speaking, the selling owner must have held the stock for three years before the sale. However, if the seller had an asset or

---

upon which the 30% threshold would have been reached, allowing the Section 1042 tax deferral to take place. However, the owner could elect Section 1042 treatment only on that 1% because, as explained below, the tax-deferred reinvestment in other securities must take place between 3 months before the sale and 12 months after, and the other 29% was sold years ago in this example.

business interest that was exchanged in a tax-free transaction for stock in the company that now is setting up the ESOP (for example, if the company was recently formed through the exchange of stock for an existing asset), the holding period of the asset will be "tacked" to the holding period of the stock, and the three-year rule will be met. Additionally, if the selling owner acquired the stock as a gift, the donor's holding period can likewise be "tacked on" to the owner's holding period to meet the three-year rule.

The stock cannot have been acquired through a distribution from a tax-qualified retirement plan or through an option or company stock purchase arrangement. For example, this means that ESOP participants who receive stock cannot elect the Section 1042 tax deferral if they sell the stock back to the company.

The Seller Must Reinvest the Gains in Stocks or Bonds of U.S. Companies

To elect the Section 1042 tax deferral, the seller must reinvest in "qualified replacement property" (QRP) during the period beginning 3 months before and ending 12 months after the sale date. QRP must consist of stocks, bonds, or other equity instruments such as debentures. It must be issued by domestic (i.e., U.S.-based) operating corporations that obtain no more than 25% of their gross income from passive investments (such as income from royalties, rents, etc.).[3] QRP does not include mutual funds, U.S. or municipal bonds, or real estate investment trusts (REITs). Securities of the company sponsoring the ESOP are ineligible, but QRP can include stock of other companies owned by the seller as long as they are not in the same controlled group of corporations as the ESOP sponsor. There are long-term floating-rate corporate securities, often called "ESOP Notes," that are specifically designed to serve as QRP.

---

3. There is an exception to the passive investment rule for certain financial institutions and for insurance companies subject to taxation.

The QRP needs to qualify as such only when the seller buys it. If the seller buys and records securities as QRP but they later stop qualifying (e.g., if the seller buys stock of a U.S. company that later reincorporates outside the U.S.), the QRP will not be disqualified.

The funds used to buy the QRP need not literally come from the ESOP transaction, so the "reinvestment" is not necessarily a rollover of proceeds from the sale, although it very often is. However, the tax that is deferred is the tax that would be paid on proceeds from the ESOP sale, so the maximum amount that can be invested in QRP is the amount coming from the ESOP sale. Note that the seller need not elect the Section 1042 tax deferral for all of the proceeds; for example, he or she can reinvest 50% of the proceeds in QRP and pay tax on the other 50%.

The Seller Must Meet Section 1042's Procedural Requirements

To qualify for the Section 1042 tax deferral, the seller must make three kinds of filings:

1. *Statement of election.* The seller must formally elect Section 1042 treatment in a "statement of election" attached to the seller's tax return for the taxable year in which the sale to the ESOP occurs.

2. *Statement of purchase.* For every purchase of QRP (remember, all such purchases must take place within the single 15-month window described above), the seller must execute and have notarized a "statement of purchase." This formerly had to be notarized within 30 days after the purchase, but the IRS currently allows it to be notarized not later than the filing of the seller's tax return for the year in which the election was made, or, if the QRP was purchased later, not later than the filing of the seller's tax return for the next year. Every statement of purchase is filed with the seller's tax return.

3. *Statement of consent from the company.* The seller must file with the statement of election a verified written statement from the company (i.e., the employer sponsoring the ESOP) consenting to the application of the excise tax provisions under Code Section 4978 (a 10% tax if the ESOP disposes of the shares from the Section 1042 transaction within three years) and Code Section 2979A (a 50% tax if a prohibited allocation is made under the ESOP).

The Seller Will Pay Tax If Any QRP Is Sold

The QRP holdings are *not* like an IRA or other tax-deferred account within which people may buy and sell without paying tax. Instead, the seller will pay tax if he or she sells or otherwise disposes of any QRP (but only on the QRP that was disposed of).[4] Thus, within 12 months after the ESOP sale, the seller must make investment decisions that he or she will live with until death if tax is to continue to be deferred. If the QRP is held until the seller dies, there will be a step-up in basis, and the seller's heirs will pay no tax.

If the QRP is a bond and it reaches its stated maturity date, or the QRP is a callable bond (i.e., the issuer can redeem it before it matures) and it is called, that counts as a disposition, and the seller will pay tax.

To get around the pay-tax-if-you-sell limitation of QRP, some sellers buy long-term, noncallable bonds and hold them to avoid paying taxes but borrow against them and invest freely in the market.

The Company Must Hold the Shares for at Least Three Years to Avoid an Excise Tax

As noted above in the discussion of procedural requirements, the company generally will pay an excise tax if, within three years after

---

4. For purposes of computing the tax, the basis of the QRP is the basis of the stock sold to the ESOP. There is no tax if the QRP is disposed of in certain transactions, such as a donation of QRP to a charity.

a transaction in which the seller elected Section 1042 treatment, the ESOP disposes of securities acquired in the transaction. However, the actual rule does not literally trace the shares sold to the ESOP in the Section 1042 transaction. Rather, the excise tax is imposed if, during that three-year period after the sale, (1) the total number of shares in the ESOP is less than the number of shares it held immediately after the ESOP transaction or (2) the value of stock in the ESOP is less than 30% of the value of all company securities as of the date of the disposition.

The rule does not apply to tax-free stock exchanges; dispositions to meet the ESOP diversification requirements; or benefit distributions made by reason of death, retirement after age 59½, disability, or a separation from service resulting in a one-year break in service.

The ESOP Is Prohibited from Allocating Shares from the Sale to the Seller, the Seller's Relatives, and More-Than-25% Shareholders

Under the prohibited allocation rule governing Section 1042 sales, when a selling shareholder elects the Section 1042 tax deferral, the ESOP is forbidden from allocating stock from that transaction to the seller, certain relatives of the seller, and more-than-25% stockholders.

For the later of (1) 10 years after the sale or (2) the date of the final allocation of stock from the sale if it was a leveraged transaction, the ESOP cannot allocate shares from the Section 1042 transaction to either selling shareholders who have elected Section 1042 treatment or to certain close relatives (siblings, spouses, ancestors, and lineal descendants).[5]

So long as shares from the Section 1042 transaction remain in the ESOP, they cannot be allocated to more-than-25% shareholders, defined as owners of more than 25% of any class of stock, more than 25% of the value of any class of stock, or more than 25% of

---

5. The IRS has ruled that if multiple sellers elect Section 1042 treatment, they are mutually excluded from allocations attributable to each other's shares.

any class of stock (or the value thereof) in a member of the same controlled group of corporations. Shares owned by certain parties such as parents, spouses, children, and grandchildren are attributed to the person, as are any ESOP-held shares allocated to the person's ESOP account, plus shares represented by stock options or similar instruments (warrants or convertible debentures). In testing for more than 25% ownership, the one-year period ending with the sale date and the date the stock from the sale is allocated are counted.

There is one exception to the prohibited allocation rule: a total of 5% of the stock from the Section 1042 transaction can be allocated to the ESOP accounts of the seller's lineal descendants. However, in many cases, the lineal descendants are more-than-25% owners by attribution and thus are excluded from the ESOP.

The company cannot use a tax-qualified retirement plan to reward employees who are prevented from receiving ESOP allocations under this rule; however, it can use equity incentives such as stock options.[6]

If the prohibited allocation rule is violated, the person in question is taxed as though he or she has received a taxable distribution of the allocation, and the company sponsoring the ESOP pays a 50% excise tax on the amount of the allocation.

Planning Considerations

Choosing Whether to Elect Section 1042 Treatment

The Section 1042 tax deferral has been a major advantage for many sellers over the years, but sometimes it is not worth using, as in the following situations:

---

6. Also note that the prohibited allocation rule applies only to shares from transactions in which the seller elected Section 1042 treatment. The ESOP may hold other shares that may be allocated to the seller, his or her relatives, and more-than-25% shareholders. However, the ESOP cannot make up the difference between these persons and other ESOP participants by contributing extra cash or other non-employer-stock assets to their accounts.

When the company is an S corporation and Section 1042 would offer little benefit. As noted above, one requirement for the Section 1042 tax deferral is that the company must be a C corporation, so an S corporation could revoke its S status and become a C corporation so the owner could elect Section 1042 treatment. One problem with this is that the company would then have to wait five years to re-elect S status, which would be undesirable in some situations. Also, Section 1042 holds little value for some S shareholders. In S corporations where distributions are relatively minimal, shareholders can accumulate a relatively high basis in their shares, meaning that there is little taxation when they sell their interest in the company. In such cases, Section 1042 is often more trouble than it is worth, especially since the company will not have the tax advantages of S status while it is a C corporation.

When too many crucial people would be excluded from the ESOP. As noted above, certain family members of the seller (except for a narrow exception), plus more-than-25% shareholders, are excluded from receiving ESOP allocations attributable to the transaction. In some cases, this is unacceptable, and the seller thus goes forward with an ESOP transaction but does not elect Section 1042 treatment.

When the seller wishes to pay tax now and invest freely without regard to the limitations of QRP and potential future taxes. The ESOP rules are very limiting for some sellers who reinvest under Section 1042 because they are limited in their investment choices (no mutual funds, for example) and because the tax deferral will end if and when they ever sell their QRP. For some people, this is a good reason to pay tax now, take the post-tax proceeds, and invest freely. Additionally, some sellers believe that future capital gains tax rates will be higher, in which case they would pay more in taxes if they acquired QRP and then sold it later on instead of paying tax now.

Seller Financing and Section 1042

As the chapter on financing in this book notes, seller financing (in which the selling owner receives a note from the ESOP for some or all of the sale price) is becoming increasingly popular. This creates issues when the seller wishes to elect Section 1042, however. Seller financing means that the seller will receive a stream of payments from the ESOP over a period of years, but the Section 1042 tax deferral is available only to the extent that the seller purchases QRP within 12 months after the transaction. If the seller does not have other funds available to invest in QRP within 12 months after the sale (as noted above, QRP need not be bought with the actual proceeds of the sale to the ESOP), then he or she cannot fully take advantage of Section 1042. This potentially means that electing Section 1042 treatment would have no value for an owner involved in a self-financed sale to an ESOP. However, the seller can borrow the money to buy QRP and then use income from the QRP to repay the loan taken out to buy it. This is usually done by buying "ESOP Notes," non-callable bonds qualifying as QRP. Banks will usually loan up to 80% or 90% of the face value of such bonds.

The Section 1042 Deferral in Mergers and Acquisitions

There is a trend in the ESOP community to use the ESOP as a vehicle for acquisitions. When an ESOP company seeks to acquire another company, the parties may desire to allow the owner of the target corporation to take advantage of Section 1042—an opportunity that would give the acquiring company a competitive edge in the acquisitions market.

The problem is that the ESOP is in the acquiring company, whereas the target owner's stock is in the target company. There are a few ways to deal with this. For example, the acquiring company can be merged into the target company in a reverse merger, followed by a sale to an ESOP by the target's owner in which he or she elects

Section 1042 treatment. Or both companies, not just the acquirer, could set up ESOPs (in which the target's owner would elect Section 1042 treatment), followed by a merger. In yet another approach, the target company merges into the acquirer in exchange for shares in the acquirer, whereupon the target's owner sells the newly acquired shares of the acquirer to its ESOP and elects Section 1042 treatment. In any case, to qualify for Section 1042 treatment, the target's owner must have owned the shares for at least three years (or otherwise meet the three-year holding requirement described above) before the sale to the ESOP.

Valuation Considerations

As the chapter on valuation in this book explains, all ESOP transactions involving company stock in a closely held company must be based on a valuation from an independent appraiser. Moreover, the ESOP cannot pay more than fair market value for the shares it acquires. The appraised price for ESOP purposes may reflect a discount for lack of control if a non-controlling interest would be sold to the plan (a majority or other interest giving the owner voting control over the company is worth more than a non-controlling interest). The appraised price may reflect a further discount for lack of marketability (i.e., since the company is closely held).

For some sellers, this may become an issue if another potential buyer (perhaps a competing business willing to pay a premium for the company) offers more money than the ESOP would pay. In such a situation, the seller must weigh the tax and other advantages of an ESOP against the higher price being offered.

Charitable Contributions and ESOPs

Many owners who sell to an ESOP have charitable intentions for at least some of their sales proceeds. Such sellers may find it advantageous to use a charitable remainder trust (CRT), a tax-exempt, irrevocable trust designed to pay out its assets to a charity. With a CRT, the seller makes a contribution of securities to the trust and in return receives a tax deduction for the contribution (in the amount of its actuarially calculated remainder interest), plus an income stream for a specified period or for life. This can provide the owner with more income than a simple donation outside the ESOP context in which the owner first sells the stock, pays taxes, and then contributes the remaining money to the charity.

One way to use a CRT is for a C corporation owner to sell to an ESOP, elect Section 1042 treatment, reinvest some or all of the proceeds in QRP, and contribute some or all of the QRP to the CRT; this contribution constitutes a tax-free disposition of the QRP. The seller then receives a tax deduction, plus a stream of income from the CRT. The charity receives a larger contribution than it would have otherwise because the Section 1042 tax deferral allows the seller to contribute all the money from the sale instead of paying taxes and then contributing the remainder.

Another way to use a CRT is for the selling owner not to sell to the ESOP at all, at least not for the amount that the CRT is to receive. Rather, the seller contributes his or her company stock directly to the CRT, which sells it to the ESOP. (This is facilitated by a prearranged understanding among the parties that this sale will occur.) Again, the seller receives a tax deduction and income stream.

Alternatively, the seller may dispense with a CRT and instead simply contribute QRP to a charity, providing both a larger contribution for the charity and a larger tax deduction for the seller. However, there will be no income stream for the seller.

The main downside of any of these approaches is that the selling owner no longer has the securities that have been contributed and thus cannot leave those securities to his or her heirs. In any case, a charitable donation works best for business owners with a serious charitable intent.

Chapter 3

ESOPs in S Corporations

Corey Rosen

The most tax-favored business form in the U.S. today is an ESOP-owned S corporation. Until 1998, ESOPs and other non-taxable entities could not own shares in an S corporation, but that law was changed so that starting in 1998, non-taxed entities could own S stock, provided they paid tax on the earnings at the highest personal rate. Congress specifically decided, however, that ESOPs, and only ESOPs, should not have to pay any tax. So if the ESOP owned 30% of the stock, tax would not have to be paid on 30% of the profits of the company; if it owned 100%, no tax would be due. This is not a loophole in the law but a considered and discussed congressional choice to encourage employee ownership.

As a result of this, there has been an explosion of S corporation ESOPs. While many of these are in S corporations that set up an ESOP to buy a minority ownership stake, the majority are 100% ESOP-owned companies, usually conversions from C corporations with ESOPs. While a few of these C corporations were already 100% ESOP-owned, most were companies that saw the opportunity to acquire this highly favored tax status, had the ESOP buy the remaining shares, and elected S status. We estimate that perhaps 40% or more of all ESOPs are in S corporations, and 20% or so of all ESOP companies are now 100% ESOP-owned. Because this topic is so important, we have placed this chapter early in the book.

Although S corporation ESOPs have unique tax advantages, they also have some limitations compared to C corporation ESOPs. The basic attributes of S corporation ESOPs are summarized below:

1. Profits attributable to ESOP ownership of S corporation stock are exempt from federal income tax. Thus, a 100% ESOP-owned S corporation becomes the only form of corporate structure Congress intentionally exempted from federal income tax.
2. Sellers to ESOPs in S corporation ESOPs cannot qualify for the Section 1042 deferral of capital gains taxes available to qualifying sellers to ESOPs in C corporations.
3. Interest paid on ESOP loans in S corporation ESOPs counts toward the maximum amount that can be contributed to the plan, whereas it generally does not in C corporation ESOPs.
4. S corporations cannot deduct dividends (or "distributions," as they are called in S corporations) that are used to repay an ESOP loan, that are passed through to participants, or that participants reinvest in company stock. S corporation distributions can be used to repay the loan, however.
5. S corporation ESOPs designed primarily to benefit one person or a small number of people, including those intended solely or principally to benefit management or existing corporate owners, will potentially be subject to severe tax penalties.

S Corporations and ESOPs: The Evolution of the Law

The S corporation is a form of business ownership in which the corporation does not pay tax on its earnings. Instead, owners of the S corporation pay tax on their proportionate share of the company's earnings at their own individual tax rates. S corporations often pay a distribution to these owners roughly equal to the amount of tax they owe. When owners of an S corporation sell their ownership interest, they pay capital gains taxes on the gain. Their basis is increased by allocations of earnings on which they have paid taxes. S corporations allow owners to avoid the double taxation on corporate earnings that must be paid in C corporations (the company pays taxes on profits; the owners pay taxes when the profits are distributed). S corporations can have only one class of stock and no more than 100 owners.

Until 1998, S corporations could not have an ESOP that owned stock in the company, because ESOPs are non-profit trusts, which could not own stock in an S corporation because the trust would not pay tax, thus allowing a portion of the earnings to go untaxed. In 1997, Congress exempted S corporation ESOPs (and, among trusts that can be S corporation owners, only ESOPs) from the unrelated business income tax (UBIT). Effectively, ESOP participants pay this tax when their shares are distributed to them (their basis in the shares would be lower than that of other owners who had paid tax, so their taxable gain would be higher), but participants have the option of rolling their distributions into an IRA and deferring tax further. The law also allows S corporations to require that departing employees take their distributions in the form of cash rather than stock, thus avoiding the potential disqualification that could occur if an employee put the stock into an IRA (IRAs and other non-ESOP retirement trusts cannot own S corporation shares).

Although these changes made ESOPs both possible and attractive in S corporations, S corporation ESOPs do not have all the same tax benefits that a C corporation ESOP has. Under Internal Revenue Code Section 1042, owners selling to an ESOP in a closely held C corporation can defer taxation on any gain they report from the sale of stock to an ESOP owning 30% or more of the company's shares; S corporation owners cannot. C corporations sponsoring ESOPs can deduct up to 25% of the eligible pay of ESOP participants to repay the principal on an ESOP loan, and interest payments on the loan do not count toward these limits. They can deduct up to 25% of eligible pay for additional contributions to the ESOP or other retirement plans not used to repay the loan as well; S corporations are limited to 25% for all defined contribution plans. Eligible pay excludes pay over $285,000 per year (in 2020; this number is adjusted upward annually), pay of employees not in the plan, and any other pay the plan document defines as ineligible. In S corporations, however, interest payments are included in the 25% limit, thus lowering the amount that can be contributed.

In both S and non-leveraged C corporations, corporate contributions to an ESOP are added to corporate contributions to other retirement plans to test for compliance with the 25%-of-eligible-pay limit on corporate contributions, but leveraged ESOPs can treat the plans separately. Also, no one can have more than $57,000 in contributions to retirement plans (as of 2020), including company and employee contributions, added to their account in any one year. The combination of contributions also cannot exceed 100% of any individual's annual pay.

C corporation ESOPs also can deduct dividends used to repay an ESOP loan, dividends that are passed directly through to participants, or dividends participants voluntarily reinvest in company stock in the ESOP. S corporations technically do not pay dividends. Instead, they make distributions of earnings to shareholders. While these may be functionally comparable to dividends in C corporations, they are not technically the same and are not considered dividends for the purposes of tax deductions. S corporations that are 100% owned by an ESOP, of course, do not need to be concerned about deductibility. They don't pay federal income tax anyway. But for less-than-100% ESOPs in S corporations, the non-deductibility of dividends could increase taxes for other shareholders.

Issues in Deciding on Whether to Use an S or C Structure

For S corporation owners considering setting up an ESOP, the ability to avoid taxation on the ESOP's share of earnings is a powerful tax incentive. Where the goal of the ESOP is simply to provide a benefit to employees, or the sellers believe it makes more sense to go ahead and pay capital gains taxes now, there may be no reason to convert to C status. There are other possible considerations, however, in deciding to stay S.

Where the ESOP Is Being Used to Buy Out an Owner

Normally, if an owner wants to sell, an S corporation will first convert to C status so the seller can defer gain on the sale. There are several scenarios, however, where owners of an S corporation may not want to do this:

1. *The seller is not the only owner.* While the seller benefits from the conversion to C status, the other owners now find any of their earnings that would have been sheltered from the corporate-level tax no longer are. If the sale does not create enough deductions to reduce the corporate-level tax low enough to satisfy these owners, they may not want to convert. Note, however, that the other owners may not face this problem if the C corporation ESOP creates enough debt or contribution obligations to reduce or eliminate the corporate-level tax. Also, earnings that would have been paid out to the owner in a S corporation could be paid out as compensation to those owners in a C corporation, creating almost as advantageous a tax situation because the corporation could deduct the compensation (note, however, that the compensation cannot be unreasonable, as defined by the IRS, and that it will, unlike distributed earnings in the S corporation, be subject to payroll tax).

2. *There are large amounts of undistributed earnings.* When the conversion to C status takes place, any earnings that have not yet been contributed to the owners must be distributed in one year or they are taxable to the owners (meaning they will be taxed twice, since the owners have already paid tax on them before).

If the company does not have the cash to do this, it could borrow money, but the ESOP may itself require too much cash to make this payout practical.

3. *Sellers plan to sell the company in an asset sale.* In an S corporation, the sale of the company's assets triggers only a single tax at the individual level; in a C corporation, the sale would be taxed at both the corporate and individual level, as income to the company and as capital gains to the individuals. The amount of the corporate tax would depend in part on the depreciation taken on the assets.

4. *The S corporation is creating losses the owners want flowed through to them.* In some situations, a company may be making heavy investments, often in real property or other hard assets, that create paper losses. These losses can be flowed through to the owners, who can deduct them at a marginally higher rate than can the company. In some scenarios, this may be desirable.

5. *The seller's basis is already very high because of taxes paid on previously undistributed earnings.* In this case, the "rollover" provision may not make much difference.

6. *There are multiple classes of stock, and it is important for the company or the ESOP to retain this feature.* For instance, if the ESOP has convertible preferred shares, changing to an S corporation would require they be converted to common shares. In some cases, this may not be practical. There is also a fiduciary issue for the conversion (whether it is in the interest of the ESOP participants as shareholders to convert) that could affect this transaction.

7. *The seller, the seller's family members, or other 25% owners are employees.* If the seller chooses to defer taxes on gains on the sale to a C corporation ESOP, neither the seller, the seller's close family members, nor 25% owners can get allocations of stock in the ESOP from those shares. But if the seller does not elect the

deferral (as would be the case if the company retains S status), these people all can participate. The allocations may be substantial and offset a large part of the potential tax deferral that is forgone.

Cash Flow Considerations in Less-Than-100% ESOPs

Where a company is 100% owned by an ESOP, conversion to an S is often a foregone conclusion. Why pay taxes when you don't have to? Barring special issues relating to converting from an S to a C, converting in 100% ownership situations is the norm. But where the ESOP owns less than 100% of the stock, the considerations are more complex.

Most S corporations make distributions to their shareholders in amounts at least large enough to cover their tax obligations. Because S corporations can have only one class of stock, if distributions are paid, they must be paid to the ESOP as well. Because the ESOP does not pay taxes, the distributions it receives can create a pool of cash that can be used to buy additional shares or pay off a loan. Any leftover distributions could be used to fund repurchase obligations. The distributions could also be used to buy more stock in the company. This would dilute the existing owners' percentage of ownership but not their value (because an equivalent amount of cash had been brought back into the company). The company would now have additional cash.

Where the ESOP owns less than 100% of the stock, special attention must be paid to cash flow issues. Assume the ESOP owns 50%, for instance, and the company elects S corporation status. Also assume the company makes distributions to shareholders in amounts at least sufficient to cover their taxes. Assume earnings of $1 million and that the personal tax rate of the owners is 40%. The company thus pays a distribution of $200,000 to the non-ESOP owners and $200,000 to the ESOP. Total retained earnings are now $600,000. If the company remained a C corporation and paid 38% state and federal tax on the $1 million earnings, it would have $620,000 in retained earnings. The payout to owners, however, will increase their basis and thus reduce their long-term capital gains obligation. If owners in this scenario did not want to pay out earnings but instead preferred to retain them for corporate reinvestment or did not want the additional $200,000 going to the ESOP, converting would not make sense.

Issues for C Corporations with ESOPs Converting to S Status

Many C corporations with ESOPs are considering switching to S status. Especially where the ESOP owns a substantial part of the company's stock, this can provide a substantial tax benefit, even reducing taxes to zero where the ESOP owns 100% of the shares. Indeed, it is arguably a duty of ESOP fiduciaries to consider such a switch. Several issues must be kept in mind, however:

- The election requires the consent of all shareholders.
- An S corporation can only have 100 shareholders (the ESOP counts as one). S corporations can have only one class of stock, with the one exception that they can have voting and nonvoting common shares. Some C corporation ESOPs use convertible preferred or super-common stock for various reasons. These may or may not be sufficiently compelling issues to warrant remaining a C corporation.
- An S corporation that uses last in, first out (LIFO) accounting and had been a C corporation before electing S status must pay a LIFO recapture tax (the amount by which the FIFO [first in, first out] inventory exceeds the LIFO inventory). This could be substantial in some cases, especially in capital-intensive businesses. If a company uses LIFO accounting procedures, there is an immediate recapture over four years of any excess inventory

(not assets) with LIFO over what would have been the case with FIFO.

- For a 10-year period after conversion, if the company sells any asset it held on the day of its S corporation election, it will have to pay "built-in gains" tax on that sale. This tax is in addition to taxes paid by shareholders.
- In S corporations, some fringe benefits paid to 2%-or-more owners are taxable.
- Net operating losses incurred as a C corporation are suspended while the company remains an S corporation. These losses may be applied against LIFO or built-in gains taxes, however.
- State laws vary, and some states may not track federal laws, so S corporation ESOPs still may have some tax obligation.
- If there could be an eventual desire or need to switch back to C status, remember that there is a fiduciary issue over whether the switch back to C would require the ESOP to get something back in return for what it has given up as an S corporation owner. The ESOP trustee will have to make a decision about whether the conversion, as proposed, would benefit the ESOP participants or whether its terms need to be modified.

If a decision to switch is made, conversion must occur within 2½ months of the end of the fiscal year. Plan participants are not required to vote on the conversion. This is not one of the required ESOP voting issues because conversion is a matter of individual S corporation owner *elections* rather than an actual vote. A company, however, can choose to have employees direct the trustee as to the voting of the shares.

Note also that the taxable year of an S corporation is the calendar year unless there is a valid business purpose to have a different fiscal year. Avoiding taxes is not a valid business purpose. One allowable exception is that if shareholders owning more than half the shares have a tax year other than the calendar year or are switching to the corporation's tax year. So if a C corporation wants to convert to S status and is more than 50% owned by an ESOP, the ESOP trustee could seek IRS approval for the S corporation to have other than a calendar-year tax year.

Operational Issues for S Corporation ESOPs

Valuation

S corporation ESOPs must pay particular attention to valuation issues. As with all ESOPs, all transactions involving the plan must be at an appraised fair market value. At this point, there is no regulatory guidance about how the special tax benefits the ESOP provides should affect the appraised value, but most practitioners agree that the tax benefits should not be counted. That's because those tax benefits are dependent on the company being an ESOP. Appraisals assume a hypothetical third-party buyer. If the buyer purchases the ESOP's shares, there would be no more ESOP tax benefits.

Distributions of Earnings

In most S corporations, distributions are made annually to owners in amounts at least sufficient to enable them to pay their taxes. Even though the ESOP does not have to pay taxes on its share of earnings, it must receive a pro-rata share of any distributions.

Distributions can also be used by the ESOP to repay debt. The 2004 tax law made it clear that distributions on both allocated and unallocated ESOP shares could be used for this purpose.

Where distributions are not used to repay a loan, the distributions on allocated shares will be treated as earnings on shares and will be allocated according to account balances. Distributions on unallocated shares can be allocated based on account balances or the company's normal allocation formula for contributions. Adding distributions based on account balances may raise issues for the distributional impact of ESOPs on newer employees because most of the benefit would accrue to employees who had larger account balances.

Some companies might want to pass distributions through directly to employees, but this generally is not advisable. These distributions will normally be subject to a 10% excise tax on "early distributions." The pass-through would also require the consent of each employee and would be subject to taxation.

Distributions of Account Balances to Departing Employees

In C corporation ESOPs, employees generally can demand distributions, and companies can choose to make distributions, in the form of company stock. Employees can roll over that stock into an IRA. However, because S corporation rules do not allow for there to be more than 100 shareholders at any one time or for an IRA to hold stock, S corporation ESOPs must follow specific procedures for making distributions. If an S corporation ESOP wants to distribute shares to employees when they leave (because the company wants to buy back the shares or for some other reason), but wants to give employees the opportunity to roll over the distribution into an IRA, a company can craft its plan so that employees can either get stock and sell it back or get cash and roll it over. If the employee only gets stock that is held very briefly—one day to allow the company to buy it back, for instance—the IRS has ruled that this does not really constitute ownership for the 100-owner test. It also does not create any potential problems with taxes for the employee who rolls the cash into an IRA. The IRS, in a private letter ruling, has confirmed the acceptability of this approach.

Alternatively, the company can just convert the shares into cash before distribution. S corporation ESOP rules specifically allow plan sponsors to eliminate the normal right employees have to demand a distribution in the form of shares.

Rules for Preventing S Corporation ESOP Abuses

Soon after the law was passed allowing ESOPs to be owners in S corporations and not to have to pay tax on their share of corporate earnings, there was a predictable (if disheartening) rush by some financial advisors to propose ESOPs for clients who really were not interested in sharing ownership broadly with employees. In some cases, this might be for professional firms with one or a few employees. In others, schemes were proposed in which managers would create an S corporation management company to manage a larger operating company. The management company would charge a management fee to the operating company equal to a large percentage of its profits. Because the management company would be structured as an S corporation owned by its ESOP, there would be no tax on these profits. In a more complex approach, the management company would include the employees of the operating company in its ESOP (this is allowable in companies that are part of the same control group). Managers in the S corporation would then pay themselves substantial deferred compensation that would escape tax because the S corporation would be 100% owned by the ESOP.

ESOP experts argued that all of these scams were already precluded under general authority granted the IRS to disallow tax shelters that have no valid business purpose other than to shield people from tax. If this test did not work, IRS regulations provide that "if the plan is so designed as to amount to a subterfuge for the distribution of profits to shareholders, it will not qualify as a plan for the exclusive benefit of employees even though other employees who are not shareholders are also included under the plan."

To provide more specific prohibitions, as well as to buttress the general language giving the IRS power to rule against these scams, Congress included a draconian set of tax penalties in the 2001 tax law.

In addition to the specific rules set forth below, the IRS developed regulations to define existing plans as subject to this legislation, regardless of when they were established, if their purpose is "in substance, an avoidance or evasion of the prohibited allocation rule."

The law is quite complex. The simplest way to describe it is to say that it provides extreme tax penalties for plans designed to funnel most of their benefits to a small group of people who own most of the company, either directly and/or through the plan or through "synthetic" equity. Synthetic equity includes stock options, phantom stock, stock appreciation rights, stock warrants, and most kinds of deferred compensation whose payment represents a claim on the assets of the corporation. It is intentionally a very broad definition. To find out whether a plan is subject to the law, two steps need to be taken:

1. First, you must determine whether there are any "disqualified persons," defined as anyone who as an individual owns 10% or more, or as part of a family owns 20% or more, of the "deemed-owned shares." Deemed-owned shares are (a) shares allocated to an individual in the ESOP, (b) the individual's pro-rata share of unallocated ESOP stock, and (c) any synthetic equity. Anyone in this group is considered "disqualified." Note that this means someone does not have be an ESOP participant to be in this group. Family members include spouses, lineal ascendants or descendants, siblings and their children, and the spouses of any of these family members. Being a disqualified person does not mean, however, that this person cannot be in the ESOP or receive synthetic equity. For that to be the case, the disqualified persons must also meet the test in step two.

2. Second, determine whether disqualified persons together own at least 50% of all shares in the company. In making this determination, ownership is defined to include:[1]

---

1. Disqualified persons are considered to own shares held by certain relatives plus a proportionate amount of shares held by certain corporations and other entities they control.

a. shares held directly

b. shares owned through synthetic equity

c. allocated or a pro-rata portion of unallocated shares owned through the ESOP

If disqualified persons own at least 50% of the stock of the company (through the ESOP, deferred compensation [including synthetic equity such as options and phantom stock], and direct ownership), there is a "nonallocation year," which means that penalties will be imposed for the excessive concentration of equity in the company among this limited group of people. These individuals may not receive an allocation from the ESOP during that year without a substantial tax penalty. This includes allocations of forfeited stock from departing unvested participants. It would also be impermissible to make up for the nonallocation by allocating more synthetic equity. If such an allocation does occur, it is taxed as a distribution to the recipient and a 50% corporate excise tax would apply to the fair market value of the stock allocated. If synthetic equity is owned, a 50% excise tax would also apply to its value as well. In the first year in which this rule applies, there is a 50% tax on the fair market value of "deemed-owned shares" even if no additional allocations are made to those individuals that year (in other words, the tax applies simply if disqualified persons own more than 50% of the company in the first year).

Conclusion

S corporation ESOP tax laws are not an accident or loophole. Congress intended this result because a large majority of its members believed that employee ownership is a valuable way to improve productivity and create a more equitable distribution of ownership. Companies that currently have ESOPs and are principally owned by their plan should almost invariably take a very serious look at electing S status. Existing S corporations without ESOPs may find setting up a plan desirable as well, especially if their owners do not want to take advantage of the tax-deferred sale to an ESOP available to owners of C corporations. For those who want to use an S corporation ESOP primarily to benefit a small number of people, while minimizing or bypassing altogether the law's intent to spread ownership broadly, the best advice is not to proceed. The rewards may seem great, but the risks are even greater.

Chapter 4

Things to Do with an ESOP Besides Buying Out the Owner

Corey Rosen

The most typical use of an ESOP is to provide a market for the shares of owners who want to sell all or part of their ownership interests. ESOPs are by no means limited to this application, however. They also can be used simply as an employee benefit plan, as a match to a 401(k) plan, to acquire new capital or other companies, to buy out a division of a company, to support the market for a thinly traded company's stock, or even, in a few select situations, to save a company that would otherwise close. This chapter looks at these other uses.

The ESOP as an Employee Benefit Plan

In many ESOP companies, the plan's purpose is simply to provide an incentive for employees linked to the company's performance. This kind of ESOP is conceptually and practically straightforward. The company typically will issue additional shares to contribute to the plan. These new shares dilute the interests of existing shareholders but also generate a tax deduction for the company equal to the fair market value of the stock contributed.[1] Shares contributed to the plan are allocated to accounts for employees in the plan as they are contributed. Like other ESOP shares, they must be repurchased after employees terminate or retire.

In setting up a plan like this, companies must consider several issues. First, these plans can be dilutive to other shareholders. The simplest way to deal with this is to set an acceptable ceiling on dilution. For instance, assume the owners agree that they can accept a 25% dilution. When this figure is approached, the company can limit future stock contributions to shares that are repurchased from departing employees. That way, the plan would always maintain a 25% level of ownership. If this level of contribution seems inadequate to meet the overall target levels for employee retirement benefits, then additional cash can be contributed to the plan so long as the plan retains most of its investment in company stock.

While this is the simplest approach, it may not be the best one in terms of employee incentives because it limits what can go into the plan to an arbitrary number. A more dynamic approach would be to look at what the company wants to contribute to the plan as a percentage of pay. In most companies with an ESOP used as an incentive plan, there is both an ESOP and a 401(k) plan. Employees can defer pay into the 401(k) plan, and the company may make an additional cash match. The company also contributes a fixed percentage of pay to the ESOP each year, based on a determination of what overall percentage of pay the company should be contributing to the ESOP and 401(k) plan to attract, retain, and motivate employees. In this model, dilution becomes a function of compensation needs. Moreover, as payroll grows, dilution will grow as well. Owners may find that acceptable, however, because the growth usually implies that they now own a smaller piece of a bigger company.

---

1. The deduction for the interest portion of the loan, however, is subject to the 30% of EBITDA (30% of EBIT in 2022 and beyond) interest income limitation for companies with more than $25 million in gross receipts.

A third approach is to make the determination of how much goes into the ESOP based on profitability or some other performance target. For example, the company might put a percentage of pretax profits into the plan each year. Usually, this percentage is calculated using one of two ways. The first method is to provide an amount that in a normal year the company would consider appropriate and meaningful. The second method is to provide an amount based on an assessment of what seems like an affordable and reasonable percentage of profits to set aside for employees. Here, too, the dilution of other owners will vary. However, because the amount going to employees grows only if the company's profits grow, it is even clearer that the owners will own a smaller part of a larger company.

Whatever approach is chosen, some key issues need to be kept in mind. First, the maximum deductible contribution to the ESOP and other defined contribution plans (401(k), profit-sharing, stock bonus, and money purchase plans) is 25% of the eligible pay of plan participants. In leveraged ESOPs in C corporations, the 25% is in addition to contributions to other defined contribution plans or other contributions made to the ESOP for purposes other than repaying the loan. Employee deferrals into the 401(k) plan do not add into this calculation. Second, contributions must be more than symbolic. While research cannot pinpoint a dividing line and say "more than this is enough, and less than this does not work," the average contribution to an ESOP of this type is in the range of 5% to 10% of pay, with many plans above this amount. Third, if the plan is to work as an incentive, employees need to know what they need to do to earn it (if there is a profit-sharing formula that triggers it) and what makes the stock price go up and down. As in all ESOP companies, a management style that shares financial information regularly and allows employees structured opportunities to share ideas and information can help achieve this goal.

If the company is an S corporation, another consideration is the required distributions that must be made to the ESOP. Like any other owner, the ESOP must receive a pro-rata share of any distributions. So if the 75% owners get $150,000, the ESOP, with its 25% share, must get $50,000. This is not considered a contribution to the ESOP but rather earnings on ESOP shares. This additional contribution could be used to buy additional company shares, buy back shares from departing employees, or simply as an additional cash contribution to employees. However it is used, it adds to employee accounts and reduces corporate cash flow. In many cases, this will be completely acceptable; in others, it will present a serious issue.

Using the ESOP to Match 401(k) Plan Contributions

Because 401(k) plans require minimum participation levels, companies often match employee payroll deferrals (typically at 25% to 75% of the contribution). The match can be in any number of investment assets the company chooses, including company stock. One way to provide this match is with an ESOP. The ESOP and 401(k) plan can be integrated into a single plan document or can operate side by side. The latter approach is administratively more flexible, although it requires two separate plan documents to be drawn up.

In the simplest approach, the company just contributes stock or cash to buy stock to a nonleveraged ESOP. The contribution may be based on what employees defer, on company profits, or a straight percentage of pay formula. In a more sophisticated approach, the company sets up a leveraged ESOP that borrows money to acquire shares. The allocation of stock from the leveraged ESOP is used to determine the match. For instance, say employees are putting $1 million into the 401(k) from their own deferrals. A leveraged ESOP might acquire 100,000 shares at $20 per share with a 10-year loan and repay 10% of the principal each year. Stock with an original cost of $200,000 per year and $20 per share per year would then be allocated as an employee match in the first year.

But now say that in year two, the stock is worth $25 per share. Now, $250,000 in stock value will be released to employee accounts. If a few years later the stock goes to $50 per share, then $500,000 would be released. Unless payroll deferrals have grown as quickly, employees will be getting a larger match to their 401(k) accounts. The actual cost to the employer will be the same $20 per share, and the amount of the contribution the company records for purposes of contribution limits will also be $20 per share. Accounting rules stipulate that the value declared for the income statement, however, will be the value of the shares when released.

Because the value of the match would vary from year to year with the stock price, the company needs to make some choices about how the match will be made. One way to do this would be to allow the matching amount to vary with the value of the shares. If the share value rose quickly, as happened in many 401(k)/ESOP combinations in the 1990s, employees would see very large matches. If it dropped, the matching amount would fall. Another approach would be to borrow only enough money so that the repayment of principal would release what would normally be expected to be a part of the matching requirement and "top off" the remainder with cash. Keep in mind that the company will eventually have to buy back the shares from employees at whatever the price is at that time.

Whether the match is leveraged or nonleveraged, the employer needs to decide whether the contribution should literally be a match to what employees defer or just should be a straight contribution. A straight contribution of 3% of pay or more, regardless of how much, if anything, employees defer, has the advantage of automatically qualifying the plan as meeting the testing rules for the 401(k) plan (it meets the "safe harbor" test). Aside from solving the discrimination problems, it makes sure everyone gets at least some ownership. By contrast, a match-only approach means stock just goes to those who make wage deferrals, and goes more to those who defer more. Of course, the employer may want to use the ESOP contribution to encourage 401(k) deferrals, in which case this outcome would be precisely what is desired. In some cases, a middle ground will be chosen with a 3% base contribution and the remainder made as an actual match.

Where stock is publicly traded, companies must allow employees to move stock matches to other investments. At least some employees will want to do this, and it may make good financial sense for them to do so. But will this mean too little stock will be retained in the plan? Closely held companies do not face this requirement, but they may want to make it possible for employees to diversify before ESOP rules require it at age 55 with 10 years of service.

One wrinkle of an ESOP/401(k) plan is that companies using the safe harbor matching contribution rule that allows companies to avoid anti-discrimination testing by making minimum contributions to the 401(k) plan must vest the contributions immediately.

Using an ESOP to Acquire New Capital or Other Companies

When Louis Kelso created the ESOP back in the 1950s, his vision was that companies would use it to finance new capital. They would borrow money to buy machinery, buildings, land, and other productive assets that would pay for themselves in extra corporate earnings. By financing the loan through an ESOP, employees would share in the additional ownership value this capital created.

In practice, this has been used less often than Kelso hoped, but it is an important part of many ESOP companies' strategies. Say that a printing company wants to buy a new $500,000 press. Normally, it would borrow the money and deduct the interest. With an ESOP, it would have the ESOP borrow the money (technically, the loan would usually go to the company, which would relend it to the ESOP). The ESOP would use the $500,000 loan to buy new shares in the company, and the company would use the $500,000 to buy the press. The company would then repay the loan by making tax-deductible contributions to the ESOP, thus deducting both principal and interest. As the loan was repaid, shares would be allocated to employee accounts. Other owners would suffer a dilution in terms of the percentage of the company they owned, but if the press proved to be a good investment, the company would gain at least as much in value as was invested (here, $500,000), so the value of their stock would not be any lower, and it could be higher thanks to the tax break and possible additional employee productivity.

Given these advantages, why don't more companies finance capital acquisitions this way? The principal explanation, of course, is that owners would rather keep ownership to themselves. Even though the ESOP could save them some tax money, the tax savings pay for only part of the cost of giving up ownership of the asset. Additional productivity gains are only possible, not guaranteed, and may not make up the difference not accounted for by the tax savings. On the other hand, if a company wants to share ownership anyway, or, especially, if it is already primarily ESOP-owned, then financing capital acquisitions this way can be very attractive.

Buying capital is one way to expand. Buying entire companies is another. The same leveraged approach described above would work to buy another company. But what if the acquiring company is a closely held company that already has an ESOP? Can the acquirer get for the owners of the target company the tax deferral advantage available to other sellers to ESOPs in C corporations?

The answer is that it is possible but requires several extra steps to be taken. These steps are described in detail in the chapter on ESOP financing. Suffice it to say here that the most common approach is the "two-ESOP" approach in which both the target and acquiring company set up ESOPs. Typically, the acquirer will have had an ESOP in place well before the transaction. The target company's owner sells to the newly established target ESOP in a transaction that may be financed by the acquirer and takes Section 1042 tax-deferral treatment. Immediately thereafter, the acquiring company's ESOP merges with the target's ESOP. Typically, the acquiring company's ESOP now owns a majority of the target's shares (because the

ESOP in the target had at least a majority). The target company's ESOP participants can now participate in the ESOP of the acquiring company (technically, because the target is a member of acquirer's control group).

At least one or two years later, the two companies actually merge. The delay is necessary to meet tax rules concerning tax-free reorganizations, although there may be specific exemptions for unusual circumstances.

Using an ESOP to Bolster the Market for Thinly Traded Community Bank Shares

ESOPs are commonly used in community banks to help support trading in thinly traded stocks. In fact, there are more ESOPs in banks as a percentage of all banks than in any other industry. A small number of banks become 100% ESOP-owned, but the large majority of ESOPs in banks own between 5% and 20% of the company. These banks often have a large number of individual or institutional owners, most of whom own a relatively small percentage of the company. Providing a market for their shares can be difficult. The company can buy back the shares, but it is an after-tax expense. Other owners may want to buy, but only on an occasional basis that will produce difficulties in matching buyers and sellers. If the stock is traded on the "pink sheets" or a regional stock market, there may not be enough activity to support more than periodic trades. This lack of liquidity will lower the share price to an amount closer to what the price would be if the company were closely held.

An ESOP can, within limits, help solve this problem. The ESOP can make annual cash contributions to the plan to buy stock or can borrow money to buy stock from owners wanting to sell. This creates liquidity in private companies and strengthens the market in thinly traded public companies. The ESOP cannot be compelled to buy shares, however. The ESOP must determine that the price is fair and that timing of the purchase is appropriate for the best interests of plan participants. That rarely presents a hurdle, however. The trustee will need a fairness opinion or appraisal to make sure the price is not more than fair market value (the stock is too thinly traded to establish a market price acceptable to the IRS). In a few cases, the bank stock may be traded in the NASDAQ; an appraisal is not needed here. Because the purchase is in pretax dollars, this can be a more cost-effective way to buy the shares, while at the same time funding an employee retirement plan.

Using an ESOP to Buy Out a Division of Another Company

This application is a variation on the capital acquisition theme. When parent companies are looking to divest divisions or subsidiaries, they often will want to find a synergistic buyer who can offer a premium price. In other cases, however, there either is no such buyer or the company offers to sell to employees, perhaps out of a sense of obligation, to bolster employee morale at other operations, or because of outside pressure.

In these cases, the employees usually form an acquisition company. The company borrows enough money to purchase the assets of the division or subsidiary. At the same time, the new company sets up an ESOP. The company reloans the money it has borrowed to the ESOP, which the ESOP uses to buy shares in the company. The company now takes the loan proceeds and uses them to buy the assets. Alternatively, the ESOP could buy the assets and exchange them for stock. Either way, as the loan is repaid to the ESOP, shares are released to employee accounts.

Structuring the ESOP is the easy part. The real questions in these transactions are feasibility and finance. For the transaction to be feasible, all the usual elements of a sensible business plan must be in place—money, markets, and management. In many spin-off situations, the division or subsidiary may not have developed a management group capable of taking both entrepreneurial and administrative leadership. The new company will also be burdened with a lot of non-productive debt that must be paid fairly quickly. Buyouts are also often hampered by the parent company's desire to compete in similar markets. The sale may be occurring in the first place because the parent does not think much of the markets the division or subsidiary serve. The best candidates, therefore, tend to be operations with solid markets or management whose lines of business are no longer of interest to the parent but whose business prospects are not so stellar as to attract other buyers. Often, there is an identifiable missing piece in these operations, such as bad employee morale, excessive overhead charges by the parent, a lack of parent interest in potentially successful ideas or initiatives from the division or subsidiary, or high labor costs that could be reduced by an ESOP in which employees take concessions. Operations that are simply losing money in depressed markets despite the parent's best efforts are almost never good candidates, while star operations can almost never be bought by employees because someone else will pay more.

The second major hurdle is finance. In most of these buyouts, equity capital is essential. Lenders are not going to lend 100% of the value of a company except in the most unusual circumstances. This equity can take many forms, and often combines a number of elements. Where a great deal of capital is needed, there are specialized investment firms that will purchase a large, usually majority, stake in these companies with the intention of selling to the ESOP over time. Management will almost always be asked to invest its own cash, as much to provide some "skin in the game" to encourage them to stay as to generate capital. High-risk lenders may provide subordinated debt, usually at very high prices. Some states will provide loans or loan guarantees. Parent companies might retain partial ownership or invest in the transaction. Finally, employees will often be asked to contribute, sometimes directly through the purchase of shares and (more often) through wage and benefit concessions.

Buyouts of this kind are expensive to organize, time-consuming, and riskier than other ESOP transactions. They also raise more complicated issues, such as allocating equity between direct investors who risk their own cash and the ESOP, which borrows money on a non-recourse basis on behalf of employees. Few investors will be willing to take a dollar in equity for a dollar in cash if the ESOP gets a dollar in equity for a dollar in borrowed money to be repaid by the company. There are ways to structure these transactions to accommodate everyone's interests, but they take a high level of expertise and can be controversial between the parties involved.

Despite all these issues, when a division or subsidiary is for sale and employees are logical buyers, an ESOP can be a very desirable solution, giving employees a chance to become owners and, in some cases, saving their jobs as well.

Using an ESOP to Save a Failing Company

In the past, one of the most publicized, but least common, applications of an ESOP was to save a failing company. Often this was a division or subsidiary of a larger company and would follow the scenario above, usually with a strong emphasis on substantial concessions, often in the 10% to 30% range. In other cases, an ESOP was used to buy a stand-alone company. The mechanisms for this kind of sale would be similar, but the management problem is usually more acute. Clearly, old management needed to be replaced, so the first issue was to find out whether there was competent new management willing to enter the picture in what would be a very uncertain new company. Although many of these companies did succeed, at least long enough to find another buyer or become successful in their own right, this use of ESOPs has almost entirely disappeared because of all the challenges it presents.

Another scenario is the one followed at a number of airline, steel, and trucking companies in the 1980s and a handful of other companies in the 1990s. Here the employees, often represented by a union, agree to take concessions in return for stock. This was the basic structure of the United Airlines transaction, although United was not in danger of failing (instead, employees saw the danger of the company breaking into four different companies, some of which would pay lower wages). In most of these cases, the plan is time-limited; the ESOP will last only as long as the concessions. During that time, employees typically are given some governance rights, commonly minority representation on the board. This approach has not disappeared but is extremely rare.

Conclusion

ESOPs are an exceptional vehicle for providing for business continuity, but, as this chapter shows, they have many other applications. It is critical to remember, however, that whatever financial objectives an ESOP is being used to accomplish, it is first and foremost an employee benefit plan. The decision to implement an ESOP, and the way it is subsequently run, must be made with an eye first toward whether the plan is good for employees. As research described elsewhere in this book has shown, plans that are run this way help companies make more money. This added productivity is, in the end, the best reason to use an ESOP.

Chapter 5

Understanding ESOP Valuation

Corey Rosen

Why Do You Need a Valuation?

There is a T-shirt in the Exploratorium museum in San Francisco with a picture of Albert Einstein in a policeman's hat. The legend on the T-shirt says "186,000 miles per second. It's not just a good idea, it's the law." If you want to have an ESOP in a closely held company, an independent, outside valuation is not just a good idea, it's the law. You must have an appraiser figure out what a willing buyer would pay a willing seller, assuming both have all the relevant information they need to make the transaction. The law is designed to make sure that the ESOP does not pay more than fair market value when it buys shares from a non-ESOP participant shareholder and that ESOP participants are paid fair market value when selling their shares back to the ESOP or the company.

Congress created this requirement to make sure that ESOP trusts are operated for the benefit of participants. Buying shares from an owner at an inflated price puts the company at risk and benefits the owner's interest at the expense of the plan participants. Many people call us at the NCEO, saying "Why can't we just use book value?" or some other formula, or perhaps the price they got in an offer from another buyer. Book value is simple, but it usually understates the real worth of ownership in most businesses. Most businesses are worth some multiple of their expected future earnings—earnings that are generated not just by assets, but by such intangibles as reputation, expertise, contacts, innovative ideas and processes, etc.

Other owners say they know that in their industry, businesses sell for an average of x times earnings or some other multiple. But your business is not likely to be average. If in using a formula you come up with a value that is just a few percentage points higher or lower than a more accurate assessment of your company's value, the costs will be much greater than the cost of a valuation. For instance, if your formula is off 3%, and your value is $2 million, then the formula is either costing you (if it is too low) or the ESOP (if it is too high) $60,000, many times the cost of an independent appraiser.

In addition, you are not simply selling your company when an ESOP buys the stock. You are selling shares in the company, and that is an important distinction. For instance, if you are selling a minority interest, the price per share is lower than if you are selling a controlling interest, because control has value. Even if you are selling a controlling interest, shares can have a discount for lack of marketability.

Because of all these factors, only a qualified appraiser can determine the right number. To make sure that the appraiser is working for the interests of employees, the law requires that the appraiser be independent, and the U.S. Department of Labor (DOL) and the courts have argued the best way to assure that is for the appraiser to be hired by the ESOP trustee (not the board, the company, or the seller) and report to the trustee.

Business owners sometimes worry that this appraised price will not be what they think they deserve or can get elsewhere. If you have a truly synergistic buyer interested in your firm, this might be true, although even then contingencies placed on the sale and less favorable tax treatment can make a lower sale price to the ESOP still a better deal. Truly synergistic buyers, however, are far less common than sometimes thought and account for a distinct minority of sales.

An independent appraisal is also essential to convincing employees that an ESOP is a good thing for them. If they believe that the ESOP is overpaying for its shares—that it is just a clever way, for instance, for the owner to take money out of the company on a tax-preferred basis—then employees are going to be very skeptical about the plan.

An independent valuation can be also be critical if there are multiple owners. If one sells for too high or too low a price, an artificial benefit or cost is created for one party or the other. In many ESOPs, sales are done in stages. Too high a price in the first stage means the shares the seller continues to hold are worth less and the company may be put in unnecessary financial danger.

Finally, having an appraisal can be a useful business planning tool. After all, the appraiser's report, which typically runs 75 pages or so, is all about comparing your business both to other businesses and to other uses for the money invested in your company. It thus provides a detailed benchmark to determine how you are doing and what elements of your strategy can be changed to improve equity value.

Who Hires the Appraiser?

The appraiser is hired by and reports to the trustee of the plan, not the seller or the board. Most trustees do not want the seller even to see the valuation report; some do not want board members to see it either, although on an ongoing basis, boards do normally get the valuation report or at least a detailed summary because it is so critical to understanding the business. While in practice the appraisal fees are normally paid for by the company, it is important that the contractual relationship be between the trustee and the appraiser. Thus, the recommendations directed to "you" below about hiring an appraiser are addressed to the ESOP trustee, and in particular an internal trustee (i.e., a company employee or committee) as opposed to an external trustee whose business it is to know these matters.

The fact that the appraiser's client is the ESOP trust, no matter who actually writes the checks to cover the fees, has important implications. First, the letter of engagement should clearly specify that the appraiser is working for the ESOP. Second, it means the appraiser is not trying to find the highest price that can be justified or, as in some tax-oriented appraisals, the lowest. Third, it should remind everyone involved that the point of the appraisal is to protect the interests of the ESOP participants by ensuring the ESOP does not pay more than fair market value in any purchase from an outside seller and that employees are paid fair market value for company shares in their ESOP accounts.

Many business owners have confidence that the appraised value will be one they are willing to sell at, often because their motivation in selling to an ESOP is only partly financial and they believe the price will reasonably reflect what their business is worth. Some sellers want to get an idea about what the ESOP will pay before doing a deal, however, and they or the company may hire an appraisal firm to determine a value on the same basis an ESOP appraiser would. That same firm may also provide advice on deal structure (seller financing, warrants, bank debt, cash in the company, etc.). If the firm is a qualified ESOP appraiser, its number will usually be within about 10% of what the appraiser hired by the trustee will determine. It is important to understand, however, that this firm should not be the same firm the trustee hires because that represents too much of a conflict.

When Must an Appraisal Be Performed?

The appraisal must be done before any sale to the ESOP. After the plan is set up, the law requires appraisals to be done at least annually, but there may be circumstances that require a more frequent appraisal. The law also requires that ESOP transactions be conducted at the current fair market value as of the date of the transaction. In practice, the appraisal comes in and it takes some time to complete the transaction, but the price would be at the appraised number.

If the ESOP is buying shares from an owner or the company, for instance, it should try to time its purchase to coincide with the most recent appraisal as closely as possible. On an ongoing basis, in an ideal scenario all transactions related to plan distributions (such as a departing employee selling shares back to the company or the plan) occur at a specific annual date that is timed as closely as possible with the annual appraisal. In practice, what this usually means is that the appraiser provides a report on a regular schedule and the plan administrator closes the plan year as soon as possible after that. That window is usually within a few months but may be longer. Statements are then mailed to employees, and transactions are completed as soon as administratively possible following the closing.

For distributions to employees, however, plans can also state that distributions will occur as of the most recent appraisal, even though that could be up to one year old. If this is done consistently, it is normally acceptable unless there is reason to think there has been a very significant upward or downward movement in share price in the interim. In that case, the trustee may ask the appraiser for a "drop-down" letter to state that the most recent appraisal is still valid or, if this is not the case, suggest an update be performed.

Who Performs an Appraisal?

The law requires an independent, outside appraisal from someone who is customarily in the business of doing business appraisals. There has never been a precise definition of what "independent" is, however. Clearly, some people are excluded—your board, your attorney, your brother-in-law, your CFO, your CPA, or anyone else with a direct financial relationship with the company. But what about your CPA firm (but not the person doing your books), or the valuation advisor who is affiliated with your attorney? Many people argue that if your CPA firm is large and can establish a "firewall" separating its audit and valuation sections, then that is acceptable.

Others contend that even this is risky. Similarly, some people say you can use firms affiliated with your advisers (such as a valuation firm that pays a fee to your attorney for referrals), but most experts would argue that is not a wise policy.

We at the NCEO strongly suggest that you pick a firm that has no other business relationship with your company than the appraisal itself. Almost all the lawsuits that result in major judgments involving ESOPs concern valuation. The law looks primarily to process, not results, in determining whether the appraisal was fair to the ESOP. An appraisal done by a truly independent, qualified firm establishes a degree of credibility not possible any other way. With any other firm, there is always the possibility that the appraisal was done with an eye toward getting or keeping the company's business for the other parts of the firm or the affiliated parties involved in other parts of the transaction. The costs will rarely be lower in using someone not truly independent, so it is best to err on the side of caution.

In the past, the decision on whether a valuation firm that has done work for the firm before the ESOP could be hired by the trustee was a matter of disagreement, but that has changed. The DOL has been very clear on this issue in recent years and is very skeptical of appraisers who have any other relationship with the company. Appraisal firms that have done work unrelated to the ESOP should be excluded. A more difficult issue is whether an appraisal firm that is hired to do a preliminary appraisal for ESOP purposes can be used for the full-scale ESOP appraisal for the ESOP transaction. A preliminary appraisal can help a company decide whether to do an ESOP and to plan for financing it. Tim Hauser, a deputy assistant secretary at the DOL, has argued that this is "road testing" the appraiser to see if a high enough price can be obtained, and says the DOL wants companies to use a different firm for the transaction than for the preliminary appraisal, one hired by the trustee. Using a separate firm adds somewhat to the cost, but it also means the preliminary appraisal may come to a somewhat different conclusion of value than would be obtained from the firm that will ultimately do the ESOP appraisal, albeit the difference is likely to be small. Given the litigation and/or DOL investigation risks of using an appraiser who has done work for the company or the seller, and the fact that ESOP valuation professionals usually come to very similar conclusions of value, we strongly recommend that the ESOP appraisal firm have no other existing or prior relationship with the seller or the company.

The other major issue in determining whether an appraiser is qualified is competence. Here there are two areas to evaluate. The first is general business appraisal competence. Anyone can be a business appraiser. No specific degree and no licensing procedure is required by states or other entities. The appraisal industry does try to be self-regulating, however.

There are a number of organizations, offering a wide variety of designations, that provide some kind of business appraisal certification. Among these are the American Society of Appraisers (ASA), the National Association of Certified Valuation Analysts (NACVA), the Institute of Business Appraisers (IBA), and the American Institute of Certified Public Accountants (AICPA). Each organization provides some kind of technical education program providing certification designations. There are so many designations now that they can become quite confusing. It is worth asking an appraiser what designations he or she has and what was required to obtain them, but making comparisons on designations alone may be difficult.

In addition to these qualifications, you should also look at experience, in-house training requirements for the firm, whether the appraiser has spoken or published on the subject, and, of course, references.

Business appraisal competence is not enough, however. As will become clear later, there are many ESOP-specific issues. These issues can have a dramatic impact on the final valuation. Your appraiser should be able to demonstrate specific experience and expertise in ESOPs. Ask for a list of ESOP clients and call them. Find out whether the appraiser belongs to the relevant professional organizations (the NCEO and the ESOP Association), regularly attends professional conferences on the subject, and has spoken or written on ESOP-specific issues. If the appraiser claims to have ESOP expertise but does not meet these criteria, look elsewhere.

How Do You Find a Good Appraiser?

As noted above, an appraiser may be chosen by the seller, board, or trustee for advice on what the ESOP might pay, as well as possibly on deal structure. The trustee will hire the appraiser for the ESOP. In both cases, the criteria for selection are the same, although an independent trustee who does ESOP work often will have a list of appraisers it works with.

Both the NCEO and the ESOP Association maintain lists of appraisers and other ESOP professionals that are available to members. Neither group endorses the people listed in the guides, but at least this provides assurance that the appraisers are involved in the relevant professional organizations. Most active ESOP appraisers will appear on both lists. Your other professional advisors usually will also have recommendations, and you should ask other ESOP companies whom they have used.

One issue to decide is whether to pick an appraiser from a large or small firm. Large firms typically have an appraisal reviewed by one or more other staff members and may have additional credibility should there be a legal challenge. Some small firms, however, have excellent reputations and also may provide for internal reviews. Generally, large firms charge more, but this is not always the case. While there is not a right or wrong answer here, size per se is probably not a critical issue when comparing firms of comparable price, competence, and compatibility.

In picking an appraiser, it is wise to interview at least two or three candidates. You will find that there are significant variations in price, experience, and appraisal philosophy. The first two are obvious things to look for, but the third may seem a little confusing. Why ask about philosophy?

Different ESOP appraisers have different approaches to key appraisal issues, such as discounts for lack of control or liquidity (these are discussed below), or in their general appraisal approach (such as whether they rely more on earnings multiples or on comparable companies). These will have a potentially significant effect on value. Initial assumptions tend to get locked into your ongoing ESOP appraisal. It will always arouse suspicion if, a few years after the first ESOP appraisal, you decide you are unhappy with the approach and choose someone else who comes in with a different set of assumptions. Your business won't have changed, but ESOP participants and the IRS may now see a very different appraisal number. At best, you have a serious communications problem; at worst, you have a lawsuit or problem with the government.

To head off such complications, the ESOP trustee or the person who will become the trustee should interview appraisers beforehand. If the ESOP trustee decides down the road that the appraisal is in some way potentially faulty, the best approach is to hire a third party to do a review of the appraisal report (but not redo the appraisal). This is fairly inexpensive. If the review is positive, then things can continue; if not, the trustee may seek some changes in approaches by the appraiser or decide to hire an alternative firm (but not the one doing the diagnostic).

These interviews must be designed to find out what approaches are going to be in the best long-term interest of the ESOP and its participants. The goal is not to find the appraiser who will come up with the highest price. Instead, the trustee should be looking to assure, as best as possible, that the appraisal will support the long-term viability of the plan and that the appraisal will use methodologies that are generally accepted by the appraisal community and the regulatory authorities. That means the price will not be so high as to endanger the company's ability to pay for it nor so low that the current sellers will not want to sell. The appraisal assumptions and procedures must also assure that future participant distributions will be at their proper value. The ultimate price must fit within the range of what reasonable appraisers could agree is not more than fair market value.

Admittedly, these are somewhat vague guidelines, but ESOP appraisal is an art, not a science. While the process cannot be exact, however, it can and must be informed. A careful discussion with the appraiser about these issues prior to engagement can avoid confusion and unhappiness down the line. Note, however, that the appraiser may (appropriately) say that an initial discussion does not provide enough information to make an assessment of which approaches will work best.

Is the Appraised Price the One the ESOP Pays?

Once the appraiser has provided a report saying what fair market value is, that is not the end of the story. Many people incorrectly assume that this is the price that the ESOP must pay. Instead, the law requires that the ESOP cannot pay *more* than this price when purchasing shares from a seller. Indeed, it is the responsibility of the ESOP trustee to negotiate the best price possible, which sometimes will be less than the appraised value.

This negotiation might take a number of tacks. In a few cases, the seller prefers to sell for a lower price, usually because of concerns about the ability of the ESOP to repay the loan or just because the owner wants to be generous. In others, the trustee argues that tax benefits to a seller to an ESOP should come partly back to the ESOP in the form of a lower price. It is the ESOP, after all, that justifies the lower price as a result of its tax advantages. In still other cases, the ESOP trustee is simply bargaining for a better deal and, given the lack of other options the seller may have, is able to exert some leverage.

These scenarios all envision using an ESOP to buy shares from an existing owner. Sometimes an ESOP acquires new shares, such as when it borrows money to purchase shares to help finance growth, or when it accepts contributions of shares. In these cases, the trustee has less negotiating leverage because the contributions to the ESOP are diluting other owners, not buying their shares. Still, the size of a loan might be such that a lower price is needed to fit within legal requirements, or owners may wish to add another bargain element for the ESOP.

In an ongoing ESOP, participant shares are always purchased at the appraised value. You cannot, for instance, offer to pay a participant a lower price for an earlier distribution.

Opinions on Deal Structure

In addition to providing a valuation, the appraisal firm might be asked by the trustee to opine on deal structure. A significant minority of ESOP transactions are financed by seller notes in part or in full. In their simplest form, these notes carry an interest rate, usually determined based on the level of risk of that loan compared to senor bank debt. Some seller notes, however, also have warrants. A warrant is the right for someone (here, the seller) to purchase x number of shares at y price (here, almost always the fair market value for the company, as determined by the ESOP appraisal) for z number of years. Sellers take a lower interest rate in return for this right. Conceptually, what is calculated here is the present value of the foregone reasonable rate of interest expressed as the present value of the option to buy shares at today's price for some years into the future.

Say that Louise and her advisors conclude that a fair interest rate is 8%. But Louise is willing to take 4%. The note is for seven years. Say that that means Louise is giving up a cumulative $1 million in interest as a result. That has a present value of about $750,000. Louise now can trade that for the right to buy a number of shares at the current appraised price equal to $750,000 for the next seven years. If they go up in value, Louise will have the company cash them in and make money; if they go down, they have no value.

Pricing warrants involves a lot of math and a lot of assumptions. The appraiser may be asked by the trustee to determine if the pricing is fair.

In a much smaller number of cases, the company will seek outside equity investors. Now the appraiser may be asked to determine whether the deal they are getting is fair relative to the deal the ESOP trust is getting.

What Does the Appraiser Need from You?

In preparing an appraisal report, the appraiser will need a lot of data from you. The more precise and well prepared these data are, the better (and possibly cheaper) the appraisal will be. The following list indicates the key items appraisers generally need, although there may be other things requested:

- Financial statements, typically for the last five to ten years, preferably audited (but many smaller companies will present only reviewed statements). Income statements, balance sheets, cash flow and capital statements, and any explanatory footnotes or other material are included.
- Budgets or projections
- List of subsidiaries, if any
- Leases and contracts
- Compensation schedules
- Prior appraisals
- Dividend history and expectations
- Legal documents
- Prior sales or offers

- Shareholder list
- ESOP documents
- Operational information, such as sales by customer, patents, departmental budgets, competitors, etc.

In addition to a review of these documents, the appraiser will want to interview management and possibly board members, suppliers, customers, advisors, or anyone else deemed to have critical information. One or more site visits will be arranged. During these interviews, any significant issues that could materially affect operations, such as a pending environmental liability, a new competitor, management changes, or a patent expiration, for instance, should be thoroughly discussed.

It is important that your financial forecasts be realistic and well-justified. Forecasts that are built from the bottom up, vetted by multiple people, and reconciled are better than those just made by the CEO or the CFO. Forecasts should be stress-tested for possible increases or decreases, and that information shared with the appraiser. Excessively optimistic forecasts underlying appraisals have been a key element in ESOP litigation.

What Is in the Appraisal Report?

Valuation reports typically run from 50 to 90 pages. The report will cover several issues. The basis for the appraisal of the company as an enterprise should be thoroughly explained and justified (for instance, if the appraiser chose to use an earnings ratio as a key element, why that was more appropriate in this case than some other methodology). Then there should be a discussion of any discounts or premiums applied to that value for the shares the ESOP is purchasing. Again, a thorough explanation of assumptions and rationale should appear. The data used for making the determination should be outlined, and any weightings or judgments used in assessing these data should be elaborated. Any special factors that affect valuation findings, such as a change in management that could reduce future value, should be covered. Reports usually also include a number of charts and tables showing different indications of value based on different methods.

In addition to these matters, the report should follow the guidelines included in the Department of Labor's proposed regulations concerning valuation. Among other things, these include a discussion of the business, its markets, and general economic considerations affecting value. The company's book value should be considered, along with any goodwill or other intangible assets and the company's dividend-paying history and capacity. The price of similar companies, if any, should be provided. Finally, issues relating to marketability and control concerns need to be reviewed. The trustee needs to show that the process for selecting an appraiser has been thorough and resulted in the selection of a legitimate ESOP valuation expert. The trustee must also show that the financials provided to the appraiser are accurate and realistic, not best-case scenarios. In ongoing valuations, the appraiser should be able to demonstrate how the repurchase obligation has been factored into the final price.

The final valuation will be a blending of these issues. Because there is no formula for valuations, however, each report will be different.

Steps in the Valuation Process: What Is Fair Market Value and How Is It Calculated?

In calculating how much the ESOP can pay, the first step is to determine how much the business is worth as an entity. There are three basic approaches used to determine this: the asset approach, the market approach, and the income approach.

Asset Approach

This is the simplest approach and one many closely held companies already use to value their shares for purchases by key employees. It is also the least used method in ESOP appraisals. In this approach, a company is assessed based on either the liquidation value of its assets or its adjusted book value. The adjusted net asset methodology approach takes the balance sheet and transforms it from an accounting document to an economic one. For instance, an asset may be fully depreciated on the balance sheet, but still have resale value on the market. Liabilities may not appear on the balance sheet because they are contingent, such as a possible environmental issue (cleaning up a landfill, for instance). Inventories also need to be adjusted for what they could currently sell for in the market. Any accounts receivable and payable not on the balance sheet need to be considered. Any intangible, but marketable, assets (such as a trade name) need to be assessed.

While these methods are simple, they are also usually wrong. People usually want to buy a business because it can yield them a return on their investment; the ESOP always looks at a purchase this way. While a company's assets are part of what creates an income stream in a company, they are only part of it. All sorts of other factors—expertise, reputation, contacts, processes, labor practices, and other issues—condition how much a company can make. The asset approach has even less relevance when only a minority stake is being sold because minority owners cannot force a liquidation of assets.

There are a few companies, however, where the asset approach may show up as one of the weighted factors. You may also see asset value added back into the final calculation of value where there are assets that could be liquidated in a way that would have a positive effect on cash flows, or are worth materially more than the reported amounts on the balance sheet. For instance, if you own a building that has substantial value in a high-cost neighborhood, but could relocate to a lower-cost area without damaging cash flow, that extra value may be added back to the final value. That could also be true for cash on the balance sheet in excess of projected needs, more commonly measured as excess working capital. To the extent that cash (working capital) or other assets are "excess," i.e., not required to generate a given level of earnings, their market value will generally add to the value estimated through earnings measures.

Market Approach

The next approach is to see what, if any, evidence there is of how much people would pay for stock in the company or comparable companies. There may be, for instance, a history of stock sales in the company, or there could be other valid offers. These offers, however, do not necessarily establish a value that the ESOP can pay.

The market approach can use the guideline company method or the merger and acquisitions method. The guideline company method estimates the value of a business by comparing the subject company to publicly traded ownership interests in comparable, or guideline, companies. The merger and acquisition method is based on an estimate derived from the value of the sale of a controlling interest in comparable companies involved in mergers and acquisitions, most of which will be private firms, often sold for private equity investors. In either case, multiples of earnings paid by investors are used to create multiples that would apply to your company.

The methods have limitations. The offers in the M&A data are for control and possibly for synergistic control. As discussed below, control premiums in ESOPs, if they exist, are more nuanced than in these markets. If the offer is from another company with a synergistic interest in the target company, it is not a useful comparison because the ESOP valuation assumes a financial buyer. If International MegaCompany can gain operating efficiencies, or eliminate competition, by buying Pete's Pizza Parlors, they will pay more for Pete's than would a buyer who could not capture these efficiencies. The ESOP is always a *financial* buyer; it must be able to justify its purchase based on the return that investment yields as a stand-alone company, although heavy acquisition activity in a given industry may influence market pricing upward and should be considered.

Better data are available from public companies (the guideline company method), but here several complicating issues arise. First, many public companies have multiple lines of business. Second, they are almost always larger, and often much larger, than the company being appraised. Third, they may have very different capital structures than closely held companies. These and other differences make direct comparisons difficult. Most business appraisers are experienced in dealing with these complications, however, so the data on stock prices in these companies can yield useful insights about the typical ratios (such as share price to annual earnings) that can be applied, with appropriate adjustments, to provide benchmarks for applying multiples to the company being valued. When using public companies, the indicated value for the company being appraised is a minority interest, freely marketable value because the share prices of the publicly traded companies represent small minority interests in the public company.

However a market approach is constructed, a company's earnings may be "normalized" to reflect how another buyer would operate the business. This is discussed in more detail below in the section on the income approach to valuation.

Income Approach

A third set of methodologies falls under the income approach. The basic theory behind these methodologies is that a buyer is looking to make a reasonable return on an investment over an acceptable period of time, given the relative risk of the investment. A theoretical willing buyer is looking at a variety of investment choices. There are safe ones with low returns (CDs, T-bills, etc.), somewhat riskier ones with higher returns (stocks and bonds), and still riskier ones with the highest returns (individual companies). It has to be this way:

the higher the risk, the greater the return an investor will demand. In buying a company, then, the investor needs to know two basic things: what the risk is and what the income flow is that will result from the investment. There are a number of ways to conceptualize these factors, but the two most common are referred to as capitalization of free cash flow and discounted cash flow.

Capitalization of free cash flow method: With the capitalization of free cash flow (FCF) method, the appraiser develops an estimate of the company's sustainable level of free cash flow. This is usually based on history and estimates of what future FCF will be. FCF is defined as follows:

```
      Net income
  +   Non-cash charges (such as depreciation)
  −   Increases in working capital
  +   Additions to long-term debt
  −   Payments of long-term debt
  −   Capital expenditures
  =   Free cash flow (FCF)
```

Free cash flow is normally used because that is the basis from which an investor can earn a return from the investment either in the form of dividends or investment of the FCF back into the business for future growth. However, some appraisers prefer other variations on the future income theme, such as earnings before interest, taxes, and depreciation.

After these numbers are determined, they are adjusted to reflect nonrecurring items and special considerations. For instance, there may have been a large one-time expense that lowered earnings (and thus FCF) in a prior year, or an anticipated one-time expense in the future projections. Very commonly the pay and perquisites of executives or other employees needs to be adjusted to reflect what the market rates for these individuals are, unless these practices will remain in place after the transaction. If the CEO is making $700,000 a year and has a company-paid vacation to France every year, the appraiser might determine that these expenses would be substantially reduced if someone else bought the company. This excess is added back to earnings if the levels of compensation will not continue into the future. Similar adjustments to earnings and cash flow are typically made before applying multiples in the market approaches as well. After analyzing historical and potential earnings, the appraiser will determine a single figure called "representative earnings."

Finally, a capitalization rate is applied to these representative cash flows. The concept here involves some complex math, but the basic idea is simple. The appraiser is trying to determine what the present value of a future stream of sustainable FCF is. The rate is derived by subtracting the expected long-run rate of FCF growth from the company's discount rate. The discount rate, in turn, reflects the rate of available risk-free investments and the risk adjustments appropriate for the fact that this is an equity investment made in a company of a certain size (there is less risk in a large company) with specific risk concerns.

For instance, an appraiser might determine that in a particular business, the expected FCF growth rate is 6% per year. The discount rate is 25%. The capitalization rate is now 19%, and this is divided into expected FCF to determine the company's value. If the next year's (or sustainable) FCF is $3 million, the company would be worth $3 million divided by .19, or $15.8 million before considering appropriate discounts or premiums. The underlying concept here is that the investor is looking to obtain a return on investment that justifies the risk. In this case, the return would be 19% on the expected annual FCF.

Discounted cash flow approach: A similar approach is the discounted cash flow method. Here the discount rate (25% in this case) is applied to a measure of FCF. Theoretically, all the earnings could be paid out this way to justify the investment, and this would provide a benchmark for determining value. Again, annualized free cash flows are determined; these are then discounted back to the present at the required rate of return or discount rate. The appraiser will add a terminal value at the end of the forecast period to complete the analysis.

The choice of method will depend on the degree to which past earnings are the best predict of future earnings. Discounted cash flow will be used when a good case can be made that the future forecasted earnings are more indicative of what the company will make.

The discount rate is determined by a weighted average cost of capital calculation. In simple terms, this is the rate of return the hypothetical buyer needs. The weighted average cost of capital is a way to look at the various components a buyer should think about in calculating that. The buyer would want to know what interest rates are (debt capital), what the yield is on equity investments (the cost of equity capital), how much the equity in the company is relative to equity plus debt, and the tax rate of the buyer, not the ESOP company. The buyer's tax rate may not be the same as the target company. That is especially true in an S corporation ESOP where part or all of the income is shielded from tax. The buyer cannot be presumed to be an S corporation ESOP but must, instead, be presumed to pay a normal corporate tax rate. That means the after-tax earnings of an S corporation will be reduced when applying the tax rate of the hypothetical buyer. In addition, a company risk factor is usually added of between 1% and 3% to reflect the additional return the buyer will need for investing in a company with this risk profile.

With either method, the value of each year's projected earnings over the next five years is progressively discounted, and the residual value of all future years after that is added. These out years become so highly discounted that they can be estimated as a lump sum. The total of these numbers is the enterprise value. Debt is subtracted from that, then divided by the number of shares. That value may be further adjusted for lack of control, lack of liquidity, and the repurchase obligation, as discussed below.

The discount rates vary over time and with a variety of factors. In recent years, discount rates of 12% to 20% have been common.

What Discounts or Premiums Apply to ESOP Value?

Whether or not any discounts and/or premiums apply to the indicated values derived using the valuation methods described above depends on numerous factors. In ESOP valuations, discounts generally fall into two categories: liquidity and control. These are discussed in more detail below. But before knowing whether to apply a discount, it first must be determined whether or not the valuation is being conducted on a controlling interest (or enterprise) basis or a minority interest basis. Then, depending on the method and data used within the valuation method, appropriate discounts and/or premiums are applied. Similarly, whether to apply a liquidity discount depends on whether the comparisons used to determine value are based on liquid or illiquid interests in companies.

Liquidity and Repurchase Obligation Issues

If you buy shares in IBM, you can sell them any time and get your money in three days. If you buy stock in Sally's Computers, there is no ready market for the shares. You might not be able to sell them for years, and you may have to settle for less than market price if you need the money and no one is eager to buy. This lack of marketability creates a discount over the price for the sale of otherwise comparable shares in a public company or shares in a closely held company about to be sold (because in this case there is immediate liquidity). So in any closely held company selling shares other than in a total sale, there is a discount over what the price would be for publicly traded shares, usually in the range of 20% to 40% depending on the circumstances, such as any restrictions on the sale of stock, buy-sell agreements, prospects of an initial public offering, dividends, or the availability of other buyers.

Many ESOP appraisers contend that the presence of the ESOP mitigates or even eliminates this discount. ESOP rules require that departing employees have the right to put their shares back to the company (or have the company fund the ESOP to do this) at fair market value. This seems to eliminate the lack of marketability.

The reality is more complicated, however. First, there must be some assurance that the company can really muster the cash to repurchase the shares. Second, the put option does not belong to the ESOP, for which the appraisal is being made, but the participants in the plan. Third, the put option applies only in a limited window of time and only when people leave the company or can diversify their accounts. That is hardly the equivalent to owning shares in a public company.

Appraisers argue back and forth on the legal and practical issues involved here. The typical discount for lack of marketability in an ESOP company, according to NCEO studies, is 5% to 10%.

In some appraisals, the liquidity discount is where the repurchase obligation is reflected. In that case, setting a liquidity discount should not simply consist of picking some round number that seems reasonable. The obligation of a company sponsoring an ESOP to buy back shares from departed ESOP participants represents a future use of nonproductive assets. This obligation means money is not available for other uses. If the company "recycles" the shares, either by contributing cash to the ESOP to buy the stock or by buying the stock directly and recontributing it to the ESOP immediately or over time, then the number of outstanding shares remains the same, while the discounted future cash flow per share declines by the magnitude of the obligation. This should produce an iterative set of calculations. The obligation will lower value, but the new lower value means a lower future obligation. The calculations keep being repeated until a solution is found. The resulting number should be a precise one, just as other elements of the valuation are, not just a "best guess."

On the other hand, if the company redeems shares and does not recontribute them, then the number of shares drops proportionately to the decreased future cash flow, producing a neutral effect on share value but reducing enterprise value.

An emerging (and we think better) practice for the repurchase obligation, however, is to calculate the amount of the obligation over the coming years that is in excess of what the company would normally pay for benefits. This results in lower projected earnings. That results in a lower value, which makes the repurchase smaller, so the calculation is run again (and again and again in what is called an iterative process) until a solution is found. This calculation is affected by how much cash is in the ESOP, recycling versus redemption policies, and other factors.

In some cases, the ESOP trust already has considerable cash, often because the company is an S corporation and has an ESOP that has received ongoing distributions, or because the company has contributed cash in addition to stock. In effect, these transfers have already accounted for the repurchase obligation in lower earnings than otherwise would have been the case, so an additional discount is not needed.

Including the repurchase obligation in the valuation requires the appraiser to have a copy of a repurchase analysis. Companies that do not go through this process, and do not require the appraiser to factor it into the final result, will overpay for the shares, endangering the future ability of the company to grow or to honor its repurchase obligation.

Lack of Control (Minority Interest) Discounts and Control Premiums

In most ESOP valuations in the past (and some still today), a company with a minority ESOP would be valued with a discount for lack of control and would get a premium when the ESOP went over 50%. The value of this was largely a matter of judgment from the appraiser. That approach has changed, however, and, especially if you are a minority ESOP, you are likely to see a more complex and possibly mathematical calculation.

The ESOP community is adopting a firmer and simultaneously more nuanced position regarding the attributes and value of "control" in ESOP transactions and valuations. Under a more nuanced framework, the appraiser typically starts by determining a value for the enterprise as a whole based on the supposition that regardless of how much the ESOP owns, the company will endeavor to use its assets in a financially responsible and optimal way. The premise is that similar to that applied to public companies, where there is rarely a singular controlling owner and the business is operated with the objective of maximizing shareholder outcomes. Executives and managers in public companies who fall short of achieving shareholder objectives on a standalone basis, whether due to suboptimal results or industry disruption (among other reasons), may find their businesses exposed to strategic events, including mergers, acquisitions, and/or divestitures, whereby the new or successor business is expected to provide superior investor outcomes that result primarily from enhanced cash flows. In contrast, if an industry player perceives opportunity in a business combination with a lesser and/or optimizable target, there will be strategic acquisitions aimed at enhancing value outcomes for all (i.e., 1 + 1 = 3). When these events occur and the underlying pre-transaction values are compared to the transaction values, there is almost universally a measurable value premium. Generally, this premium results from the expectation that cash flows and the resulting investor outcomes from a business combination will be superior to that of a standalone going concern, even under the presumption that the standalone enterprise is already reasonably optimized.

The increasing, if not consensus, view of the ESOP valuation community is that the use of control premiums in their legacy form and magnitude likely result in valuations that reflect efficiencies and/or synergies associated with strategic control value. In doing so, these valuations likely reflect value in excess of fair market value and are thus at risk for being labeled "prohibited transactions" using conventional ESOP regulatory interpretations. If an ESOP valuation contains explicit strategic treatments to cash flows or the implied equivalent by way of an excessive control premium, the value is likely overstated and potentially problematic for the transaction and/or the ESOP's future sustainability. While such synergies and efficiencies might be available in a marketplace of motivated investors, such treatments are not directly relevant to fair market value in the normal course of an ESOP company that remains an independent going concern on a standalone basis.

If a closely held ESOP company whose valuation begins with a financial control model for the company as a whole (or something constructively similar) has an ESOP that owns less than a controlling interest, then the valuation for ESOP purposes may require discounting to reflect the additional value captured in the underlying model. But the economics of control can get foggy and require nuanced understanding and careful consideration. For example, company bylaws may require a supermajority for certain decisions. So even a majority ESOP trustee may not have full control, and there could arguably be some potential discount for that, but not as much if the ESOP had no control rights at all.

Another critical issue is that the DOL has been skeptical about the argument that an ESOP trustee has full control even with supermajority or 100% ownership. For instance, if the seller is on the board, does that mean the seller retains some control? In itself, it probably does not, especially if the seller is no longer the CEO and there are outside board members. But what if the seller is the CEO and the majority of board members are his or her employees? Or what if the seller has covenants on the ESOP loan restricting the use of cash flow before a seller note is paid? These factors and others might lead to an analysis of partial control. The challenge of quantifying the effects of governance and differentiating values as a result of form over economic substance is not unique to ESOP valuations and quite frankly may never be fully resolved. The remedy for overcoming the questions surrounding control and its varying shades of gray are likely in the substance of the transaction terms and consideration, thus removing as many doubts as possible about the pro forma economics and cash flows that will affect the ESOP company's performance after an ESOP transaction.[1]

The Impact of Leverage on Valuation

If the ESOP borrows money, it will have an impact on valuation. The interest expense on the new debt the company now has taken on to fund the ESOP will show up on the balance sheet and, in any event, represents a significant non-productive expense. While this generally will not reduce value dollar-for-dollar (there are ESOP tax benefits, the company may grow, and there is a discount for the future value of money), it will reduce the post-transaction value. This effect will disappear as the loan is repaid.

This impact is important for two reasons. First, employees need to understand why this drop occurs. Their own account values start at the lower value and thus are not reduced by the debt (unless the loan is to a previously existing plan), but they need to understand the issue to avoid communications problems. Other owners will also see their share price drop, of course. If they plan to sell before the ESOP loan is repaid, this could present a problem. In some cases, companies arrange for pro-rata sales from owners to avoid this issue.

S Corporation Issues

When the ESOP trustee receives a statement of the pro-rata share of earnings on which taxes would be paid each year, the trustee can ignore it. ESOPs do not have to pay tax on their share of the S corporation's earnings. Clearly, S status with an ESOP can enhance

---

1. Tim Lee of Mercer Capital contributed valuable editorial suggestions on this section.

earnings, yet, just as clearly, a potential willing buyer would be unlikely to maintain the ESOP. So from that buyer's standpoint, the future earnings would be unaffected by this special tax benefit. As a result, the standard practice in ESOPs is to not "tax effect" the earnings. However, over time, the tax savings will help the company grow faster and more profitably.

Conclusion

The requirement to have an ESOP appraisal is designed to assure that the ESOP process is fair to all parties involved. While many business owners would prefer to set their own prices using a formula or a number derived from prior offers, these simplistic approaches rarely result in the price the ESOP would pay as a financial buyer. ESOP trustees, as well as owners, managers, and employees of ESOP companies, need to understand the valuation process well.

Chapter 6

Financing an ESOP

Corey Rosen

ESOPs can be a very appealing way to transfer ownership to employees, but they can do that only if the ESOP can come up with a way to acquire the shares. In the simplest model, the company can fund an ESOP by contributing shares directly to the plan. That provides a good employee benefit, but most ESOPs are used to buy out one or more owners or for business expansion. To do that, the ESOP needs a source of cash. Many people we talk to approach ESOPs with the assumption that this can (or maybe should) come directly from employees, whether through direct purchases or moving other retirement plan assets into the ESOP. While this is possible, it is complicated and expensive to do, and it may impose more risk on employees than employees should or are willing to take on. Instead, ESOPs are financed primarily in one of three ways:

1. The company makes periodic cash contributions to the ESOP to enable it to buy shares.
2. The company borrows money from an outside lender, then re-loans it to the ESOP. The company contributes cash to the ESOP to repay the loan. This two-stage approach has a number of advantages, as explained later.

This chapter draws significantly on Mary Josephs and Neal Hawkins, "ESOP Underwriting Considerations," chapter 7 in *Leveraged ESOPs and Employee Buyouts,* 6th ed. (NCEO, 2013), and Kenneth E. Serwinski, "Financing the Leveraged ESOP," chapter 3 in *Selling to an ESOP,* 11th ed. (NCEO, 2020).

3. The seller takes a note. The note is to the company; the company loans money to the ESOP and makes cash contributions to pay it back. This is the same kind of two-stage transaction as with an outside lender.

If one or a combination of these three methods is insufficient, then the company may seek outside investors who will purchase some of the stock or purchase equity rights, such as warrants, to complete the deal.

This chapter looks at the various approaches to ESOP financing. While we cover the basic practices, there are many variations on these approaches. Creative lenders and advisors may be able to come up with alternative approaches. The chapter is organized as follows:

- Financing ESOPs without using debt
- Mechanics of ESOP debt financing
- Uses for ESOP debt
- Bank financing
- Seller financing
- Mezzanine financing and bond markets
- Equity investments

It is important to note at the outset that ESOPs are not a magic wand to raise money. Companies that do not have solid financials, or very good reasons to think that they will produce them in the immediate future, are rarely good ESOP financing candidates, any more than they are good candidates for any other kind of financing.

Financing ESOPs Without Using Debt

By far the simplest way to finance an ESOP is for the company to make cash contributions to the plan, which the plan then uses to buy company stock. These contributions can be for up to 25% of the eligible pay of plan participants in both S and C ESOPs. If the company has other defined contribution plans, company (but not employee) contributions to these plans will reduce this percentage dollar for dollar. Within these limits, the contributions are fully deductible.

This approach works well for companies looking to buy one or more owners out over time. It also works well if the company prefers not to borrow money, does not have the debt capacity, or wants to fund the ESOP on the basis of annual profits rather than paying a fixed amount as required by debt repayments.

The disadvantage of this approach is that many owners want to take advantage of the Section 1042 tax deferral options available to owners of closely held C corporation shares. To qualify, the ESOP must own 30% or more of the company's stock. Even contributing at the maximum percentages, it could take some years before reaching this level. One alternative is for a company that knows it will want to buy out an owner in the future to contribute cash to the plan but not use it to buy shares until there is enough to buy 30% of the stock. While an ESOP must, by law, be "primarily" invested in company stock, most advisors agree that if the plan states that the intention is to invest in company stock when enough cash is available to reach the 30% level, and that this will occur within two or three years, the IRS will not object (and, indeed, we are not aware of there having been any objections, even in plans that did not buy stock for a longer period of time). It would be advisable in these circumstances to provide the ESOP trustee with a right of first refusal to purchase any shares offered for sale and an option to buy shares once the 30% threshold is met.

In some cases, companies will accumulate cash over one or two years, then borrow the remaining amount to get to the 30% level or whatever level is desired. Once a company does have a loan, it can also make additional cash contributions to the plan. For instance, a company may borrow a conservative amount with the intention of making additional contributions if earnings allow.

Mechanics of ESOP Debt Financing

About three-quarters of ESOPs are funded with borrowing. A variety of rules apply to these loans. In almost all ESOP loans, the lender loans money to the company (the "outside" loan), which the company then reloans to the ESOP (the "inside" loan). This internal loan is, in a sense, not real money. The ESOP trust owes a certain amount of money to be repaid over a certain number of years. The company puts cash into the plan each year to, in effect, repay itself. The real debt impact where company cash goes out of the company is the external loan. While the lender could loan directly to the ESOP, the only collateral the ESOP can offer is the stock itself and any earnings on the shares acquired by the loan. The lender wants a better source of collateral than that. The outside and inside loans do not have to have the same terms. The internal loan must meet the fiduciary standards for ESOPs, however. For example, the lender (who may be a bank and/or the seller through a note) usually wants to be repaid over 5 to 7 years. If the company does well, it may repay even faster. If the inside loan had the same terms, all the shares would be released from the suspense account over that same time. That may mean putting a very high percentage of pay into the plan each year until the loan is repaid, then not having more shares to allocate to employees other than those from repurchases of departing employees. A more sustainable approach is to spread the internal loan over a longer time, often 10 years but sometimes as much as 20 years or even longer.

While the term of the inside loan can be and usually is longer, the fiduciaries must be able to show that extending the loan is for the benefit of plan participants. This could be because the loan repayments on the terms of the external loan would exceed the maximum allowable amounts that can be added to employee accounts each year, or, more commonly, because the extension of the loan terms keeps contribution levels at sustainable levels and provides for shares to be allocated to future new employees. A loan that has the effect of reducing annual contributions to a very low level, however, would potentially disqualify the plan as not being structured primarily for the benefit of employees. Also, while technically the employees do not have to start getting distributions until after the loan is repaid (except for certain employees meeting a combination of service and age requirements) it is highly recommended that distributions start as if the loan were repaid after not more than 10 years.

Each year, as the loan is repaid, a percentage of shares held in the ESOP trust equal to the percentage of the loan that has been repaid that year is released from what is called "the ESOP suspense account." The shares are then allocated to employee participant accounts based on the company's allocation formula (such as relative eligible pay). In C companies, tax-deductible dividends can also be used to repay an ESOP loan, as can distributions in an S corporation. S corporation distributions are not tax-deductible, however. The dividends or distributions paid on allocated shares must release a number of unallocated shares with a value at least equal to the dividend or distribution. Distributions or dividends on unallocated shares would release the number of shares paid for. If the share value has fallen from the purchase, this means more shares than are being paid for in terms of the loan payment must be released. For distributions or dividends paid on allocated shares, the company must release unallocated shares based on relative share balances of participants; for dividends or distributions paid on unallocated shares, the shares can be allocated either on relative share balances or the company's normal allocation formula.

The company can use one of two formulas to calculate the percentage of the loan that has been repaid: the "principal-only method" or the "principal-and-interest method." The principal-only method releases the percentage of the shares that is equal to the percentage of the total principal paid. This method cannot be used unless the payments of principal and interest on the loan are no less rapid than level annual payments of principal and interest over a 10-year loan, using standard amortization tables to determine allowable interest rates. The principal-and-interest method releases shares based on the following formula:

$$\begin{matrix} \text{Number of shares to be released and allocated} \end{matrix} = \begin{matrix} \text{Number of shares in account before release} \end{matrix} \times \frac{\text{Principal and interest payments for the year}}{\begin{matrix}\text{Principal and interest payments}\\\text{remaining on the loan, including}\\\text{those for the current year}\end{matrix}}$$

The number of shares held in the suspense account just before the release is multiplied by a fraction, the numerator of which is the principal and interest payments for the year and the denominator of which is the principal and interest payments remaining on the loan, including the current year. In other words, shares are allocated based on the total amount of the remaining loan (principal and interest) paid that year. The number of years on the loan must be fixed, not variable; renewal or extensions of the loan cannot be considered; and the interest rate is the rate that applies at the end of the year involved. The principal-only method releases shares more slowly, in most cases, and is often preferred by banks.

The contribution limits for leveraged ESOPs depend on whether the company is a C or S corporation. As discussed in chapter 1 under "Limitations on Contributions," there are two limits to consider: the amount the company can contribute to the plan (and other defined contribution plans) overall and the maximum annual addition to any one employee's account. The amount of the principal repaid is used to calculate the value of the employer contribution for the "annual addition" calculation. If the stock value rises, this means the amount added to an employee's account will be greater than the amount the company paid for the shares that is used for purposes of the limitation calculations. The IRS also allows companies to use the value of the shares released, however, if the share value is lower. Companies must choose to use the method in advance and use it on a consistent basis.

In C corporations, the total company contribution limit is 25% of eligible pay to repay the principal each year. (As chapter 1 notes, this can be counted separately from other contributions to an ESOP and other defined contribution plans.) Companies can also pay "reasonable" dividends on ESOP shares to go beyond this limit. "Reasonable" has not been specifically defined but should not be much in excess of what similar companies might pay on similar earnings. This limit is not affected by contributions to other defined contribution plans. No one participant can receive more than 100% of eligible pay in one year as an annual addition, or $57,000 (as of 2020), whichever is less.

S corporation rules are more limiting. Interest payments and forfeitures do count toward the 25% of pay limitation. Distributions on shares can be used to go above the limits, but, as noted above, they are not tax-deductible.

Note that the leverage will have an effect on company value. After the loan, the price per share will decline. While the decline may not be dollar-for-dollar with the size of the loan (primarily because of ESOP tax benefits), it will reduce the value the stock would have had without the leverage until the loan is repaid. Very successful ESOP companies may see their stock recover quickly if employee productivity goes up, but this is not predictable or reliable. This effect is especially important in two circumstances: when there are other non-ESOP owners and in second-stage ESOP transactions.

Non-ESOP owners may be distressed to see that the sale of stock by their partners has hurt their stock value. Some companies have the owners sell pro-rata to deal with this; in other cases, the problem is avoided because the other owners are not looking to sell right away anyway.

In second-stage ESOP transactions, existing employees see the value of their accounts decline. For employees who may receive a distribution before the loan is repaid, this can be painful. Some companies deal with this by providing a floor-price guarantee for the shares until the loan is repaid. That needs to be properly structured to avoid potential fiduciary issues.

Uses for ESOP Debt

Most ESOP loans are used to buy out one or more owners of closely held companies. The ESOP uses the borrowed funds to buy shares from the owner(s), who, if they qualify, may elect the Section 1042 tax deferral and invest in qualified replacement property (see the chapter on selling to an ESOP in a closely held company for details). ESOPs can also be used to acquire new capital, buy other companies, or refinance existing debt.

When an ESOP is used to acquire new capital, the company issues new shares and sells them to the ESOP, which borrows money to purchase the shares. The company takes the proceeds of the sale and buys the new machinery, real estate, intellectual property, or other investment. The loan is then repaid in pretax dollars by making contributions to the ESOP. ESOP creator Louis Kelso actually envisioned this as the primary application of ESOPs, although in practice it is used only occasionally. The same technique could be used to refinance existing debt.

A more common application is to use the ESOP to buy another company. The structure here is somewhat complicated, but many ESOP companies, especially 100% S corporation ESOPs (i.e., S corporations wholly owned by their ESOPs) that have paid off their initial acquisition debt, are now doing this. In the most common approach, the target company is either a C corporation or an S corporation that converts to C status. This allows the seller to elect the Section 1042 tax deferral on the sale. To meet IRS rules that make this transaction favorably taxed, a "two-ESOP" structure is commonly used.

Typically, the acquirer will have had an ESOP in place well before the transaction. The target company sets up an ESOP. The target company's owner then sells to the ESOP in a transaction that may be financed by the acquirer and takes Section 1042 tax-deferral treatment by reinvesting in qualified replacement property. Immediately thereafter, the acquiring company's ESOP merges with the target's

ESOP. Typically, the acquiring company's ESOP would now own a majority of the target's shares (because the ESOP in the target had at least a majority), so that the target company ESOP participants can now participate in the ESOP of the acquiring company because the target is a member of acquirer's control group.

The details of this approach are beyond this book; our book *Leveraged ESOPs and Employee Buyouts* explains this and other approaches commonly used.

A 100% ESOP-owned S corporation may also simply borrow money to buy the target, not attempting to get the seller tax-deferral treatment. The employees of the target would then commonly become participants in the ESOP. Because a 100% ESOP-owned S corporation does not pay federal, or usually state, income tax, it would not be concerned about maximizing its own tax benefits by using the ESOP to take on the debt.

Bank Financing

ESOP companies often borrow money from banks, although seller financing has become much more common in recent years. Less often, ESOPs borrow from mezzanine lenders or the bond market.

Traditional ESOP financing is accomplished with senior credit from a bank. Banks do not receive any special incentives to loan to ESOPs but may be more receptive to ESOPs because their tax benefits can enhance the borrower's cash flow. Many banks are not familiar with ESOPs, however, and some may not want to make such a loan. In general, however, companies that have feasible transactions do not have difficulty finding lenders.

Banks will make the same kinds of assessments of loan quality they do with any transaction acquiring non-productive debt. They will focus on the "four c's": capital, character (management and credit history), collateral, and cash flow. In some cases, to assure that key management remains committed to the transaction, and/or to provide some additional up-front equity, lenders may require managers to make an investment. In some cases, that will be a purchase of common stock; in others (especially 100% S corporation ESOPs), it will be for some kind of stock right.

Looking at cash flow, a lender will want to have a ratio generally between 1.25 and 1.75 times the debt obligation. This is a general range, and it will vary up or down depending on economic circumstances and how aggressive the particular lender is. The bank will also want to be sure that the company can add additional debt to finance operations, if needed.

Collateral presents a potentially trickier issue. As noted, banks are not interested in having the ESOP stock as collateral. If the loan is to purchase another company or invest in new assets, this will serve as the primary collateral, but the bank will probably discount the value of the asset and seek additional coverage. If the loan is to purchase existing shares, the bank will seek collateral both from company assets and, preferably, from the seller. In many ESOP transactions, the seller reinvests in qualified replacement property, which the bank will seek as collateral. Sellers will want to negotiate a reduction in this collateral obligation as the loan is repaid. There are many variations on how this is done, such as accelerating the release if the company's EBIDTA exceeds a certain level. All of this is a matter of negotiation, however.

In assessing corporate collateral, various assets will be discounted differently. Accounts receivable, for instance, might be discounted only 20%, while inventory and the book value of fixed assets might be discounted 50%.

It is important to understand the effect of the ESOP on the company's balance sheet. The ESOP shows up as corporate debt. When the debt is recorded on the balance sheet, an equal and offsetting debit is recorded in the equity section as a "contra-equity account." It has to appear here because the ESOP loan does not show up as an asset in the asset section (although if the company is using the loan to buy a productive asset, that asset will appear on the asset side). This contra-equity account is eliminated as the ESOP debt is paid. The amount of the release is equal to the number of shares released from the ESOP suspense account and allocated to participants. Because of the way this process works, the amount by which the contra-equity account is reduced will not necessarily equal the amount by which the debt is reduced. Banks will use this ESOP-adjusted balance sheet number to calculate coverage ratios. In some cases, this accounting procedure could result in a negative number, which could raise legal issues for lenders under fraudulent conveyance laws. Companies need to work closely with lenders to make sure they understand how ESOP accounting works. When they do understand it, experience indicates they may be more willing to go beyond normal coverage ratios.

Some of the specific financial measures and ratios lenders look for include cash flow (requiring a minimum of EBITDAE—earnings before interest, taxes, depreciation, amortization, and employee benefit expense), debt service coverage (the ratio of EBITDAE to all required payments to the lender), leverage (senior debt to EBITDAE), interest coverage (EBITDAE to interest expense), and fixed charge coverage (EBITDAE to fixed charges). Again, all this is something that is negotiated and varies from transaction to transaction.

Banks will also usually place certain covenants on the loan. For instance, in a C corporation they may require that dividends, if issued, only be used to repay the ESOP debt. In an S corporation, they may require any distributions paid to the ESOP to be used for the same purpose, rather than just added to employee accounts. They may also require that the company not start repurchasing shares, except as legally required for retirement, death, or disability, until the loan is repaid. This is allowable in C corporations, but it appears that it is not in S corporations because the law does not specifically state that S corporations are eligible for this deferral of distribution to terminated employees. Audited financial statements are also usually required. There may also be restrictions on bonuses, compensation, and capital expenditures.

Because of all the bank requirements, it is very difficult, and usually impossible, for an ESOP to buy 100% of a company in a single transaction financed by a bank. Instead, most ESOPs proceed in a series of steps to reach the final percentage ownership goal or, if they want to go 100% in one transaction, rely on seller financing.

The term of an ESOP loan is typically 5 to 7 years, and rarely longer than 10 years. This is for the "outside" loan; provided an extension of the inside loan is judged by the ESOP fiduciary to be in the best interests of plan participants, the loan can be longer.

Seller Financing

More and more ESOP transactions are being funded by sellers taking a note. In some cases, the seller financing is in addition to bank financing, in which case it is usually subordinated to it. Usually, seller financing is structured with the outside-inside loan structure described above. The seller has the company repay the note; the company loans the money to the ESOP. The added flexibility this provides may be especially important in seller financing. For instance, if the company is experiencing difficulties, the seller might forgive a loan payment or accept interest only; this would be possible, but more complicated, with an ESOP loan. The terms of the loan to the ESOP should be arms-length equivalents (similar to terms for a bank loan) or more favorable to the ESOP.

Seller financing has become more popular for four reasons. First, it is simpler to leave the bank and all its legal and financial requirements out of the picture. Especially if the bank is requiring qualified replacement property as collateral, the seller may see little difference in the risk between a bank loan and a seller note. Second, in the past, C corporation owners wanting to defer taxes found seller notes made the process difficult, for reasons explained below, although now techniques are available to solve this problem. In any event, with relatively low capital gains taxes, many owners have not wanted to take advantage of the Section 1042 tax deferral, even if they qualify, while other owners cannot because their company is an S corporation, and they do not want to convert to a C. Third, bank restrictions on the amount of leverage a company can take out mean that the percentage of the company that the ESOP can buy can be limited. Finally, in today's market, many owners find that the interest rate on the note is an attractive investment relative to other possibilities.

There are, however, drawbacks to seller financing. If the company defaults, the seller gets the company back. Sellers may need to stay more involved with the company as a result, often insisting on covenants similar to banks, as well as a board role, to protect their interests. Second, if the seller does want to defer taxation on the gain, the techniques available are somewhat more limiting in terms of investment strategies. Finally, for all their requirements, bank loans do impose a rigorous process of analysis to make sure an ESOP loan really is feasible.

Using Seller Financing When the Seller Wants to Defer Taxation on the Gain

If a seller loans to an ESOP, he or she may not be able to take full advantage of the Section 1042 tax deferral, which allows them to defer tax by reinvesting in other securities. The law specifies that a seller to an ESOP has 12 months after the sale and 3 months before it to reinvest the proceeds in securities of qualifying companies. In a seller-financed transaction, the seller may be getting paid in annual installments. The seller cannot just reinvest these installments as he or she receives them and qualify. Instead, only the amount actually reinvested during the 15-month period qualifies. As a result, the seller must have other funds to reinvest within the reinvestment period to make this work.

There are, however, techniques that make this possible. The seller would first take out a loan from a bank to buy a long-term noncallable bond that qualifies as replacement property (these special securities are called "ESOP Notes" and can be found through your advisors). Generally, banks will loan for up to 90% of the face value of these bonds because they are so secure. Then the seller uses the proceeds of the ESOP Note to repay the loan to the bank. The bond interest rate is usually low, just somewhat above the London Interbank Offered Rate (LIBOR). The loan from the bank would carry a higher interest rate, but the ESOP Note would probably carry a still higher rate because of its added risk.

There are a number of long-term (30- to 60-year) non-callable bonds specially designed for the ESOP rollover investment. Because they are non-callable (the issuer cannot buy them back at its discretion), the buyer can feel secure that they can be held until death without triggering a "disposition," as a call would be considered, and having to pay tax. The ESOP Note, as it is repaid, can usually be borrowed against to generate cash. The borrowed funds can then be used to buy and sell whatever the buyer wants. The buyer pays tax when these investments are sold, but only based on their increase in value.

This strategy may or may not be attractive. As noted, the long-term bonds typically pay a variable rate lower than other long-term interest rates. The loan interest rate to buy the bond is often somewhat higher than the bond interest rate (the loan rate is usually fixed, so its relationship to the bond interest rate varies, but it would typically start at a point or so higher). The seller can partially offset this low-return investment by borrowing against the bond as the loan is repaid to buy higher-yielding investments. Contrast that with using the proceeds of a bank loan to invest in whatever portfolio of qualified property the seller chooses and holding on to that portfolio long term, or buying an ESOP Note with cash up front and borrowing up to 90% of it to buy and sell other investments right away.

Of course, all this matters only if the seller cares about the tax deferral. If that is not the case, the seller just pays capital gains tax on the proceeds of the seller-financed sale and does whatever he or she wants with the money. The seller, 25% owners, and family member can then all be in the ESOP, something that is not the case if the tax deferral is chosen. Moreover, the Section 1042 tax deferral is available only to sellers in C corporations.

Mezzanine Financing and Bond Markets

The large majority of ESOP transactions rely on senior credit or seller financing without any additional financing. In some cases, however, this is not sufficient to buy as many shares as the sellers desire to sell. In others, lenders may require some equity investment, employees may want to buy shares, or the sellers may insist that management purchase into the transaction.

If additional debt is needed, mezzanine lenders would often be sought. Mezzanine debt is subordinate to senior credit and therefore carries a higher (sometimes much higher) interest rate. These lenders may also want the right to convert some of the debt to equity. For instance, a loan might be structured so that part of it is repaid as straight debt and part as an equity claim that kicks in at a defined future point, either in years or when a certain target is met. In these cases, companies should negotiate for a lower interest rate than would be the case with straight debt. The equity conversion feature can also be structured so that the lender sells the conversion right back to the company before ever actually acquiring shares (such as would typically be the case with a warrant). Mezzanine lenders are typically investment firms. Your banker or attorney may be able to help locate these providers, but larger transactions might require the services of an investment banker. Investment bankers place financing with private sources, charging a percentage of the financing as a fee.

The bond market is another alternative, but it is practical only for very large transactions. Historically, very few ESOP transactions have sought financing from the private bond market. Placing these bonds requires an investment banker, a "road show" to sell the offering, and compliance with securities rules.

In rare cases, state or local governments may also provide financing or financial guarantees. Most often, state or local governments will get involved only where there is potential significant job loss and sufficient private financing cannot be found. Governments may subordinate their position on the loans but not charge mezzanine debt rates, or they may act as a guarantor of a loan. Over the last two decades, however, there have probably only been a few dozen instances of government involvement. The federal Small Business Administration can also provide loan guarantees for ESOPs for loans under $5 million.

Equity Investments

Outside Investors

If outside equity investment is needed, ESOPs can look to all the same sources any company can, such as institutional investors, specialized private equity firms, venture capitalists, "angel" investors (individuals looking to make investments in higher-yielding ventures), and friends and family.

Equity investment in ESOPs poses some special challenges, however. Many equity investors would argue that because the ESOP is buying shares with a non-recourse loan, while they are buying shares with their own money, more shares per dollar invested should be allocated to the equity investors. The U.S. Department of Labor, however, has not agreed with this approach. Advisors have come up with various ways to create fairer ways to allocate equity in these deals, but companies seeking to do this need to seek highly experienced professional advice. In general, outside investors in an ESOP prefer mezzanine debt to actual equity, partly because of the limitations on how multi-investor transactions with an ESOP can be structured. Whatever technical solutions are found, however, ESOP equity investors have to understand that the ESOP fiduciary is required to negotiate the best possible deal for the ESOP. This added uncertainty has made it more difficult for ESOPs to find outside equity partners, although certainly not impossible.

Employee Investors

A more available source is management. Banks occasionally require management to buy into a deal, while in other cases managers either want to invest or sellers require it. The same fiduciary rules apply to their investment as to outside equity investors. In our experience, however, managers usually buy in to ESOP transactions at the same price as the ESOP, not seeking any special treatment. Where managers do buy in, they would usually end up with somewhere between 5% and 20% of the shares sold. These investments must come from after-tax dollars. Companies can loan the money to managers, but interest rates not considered at arms-length terms are taxable. Managers can also purchase equity rights, such as stock appreciation rights or phantom stock. Both need to have fair values set by an appraiser to comply with fiduciary rules. Both approaches also need to comply with deferred compensation taxation rules, although this should not present any difficulties for properly drafted plans.

Employees more generally can also become investors. In rare cases, employees have been asked to purchase shares individually. While this is possible, it is often impractical. Companies must comply with securities law requirements. Offers to sell 15% of the equity of a company in a 12-month period can receive an exclusion from costly and burdensome securities registration rules, but substantial financial disclosure will be required. If the company has more than $10 million in assets and the sale results in 2,000 or more total owners of the company, or 500 or more owners who are "unaccredited investors" (the ESOP only counts as one investor, however), then the company is *de facto* a public company and subject to securities laws. Shares received from employee compensation plans in transactions exempt from securities registration (such as those under Rule 701) are not included in the calculation of owners. Moreover, employees must use after-tax money to make the purchases, and the amounts that can be raised often do not justify the costs and risks involved.

A more common scenario would be to use existing retirement plan assets, typically money in 401(k) plans or profit-sharing plans. Most 401(k) plans have two parts: the part made up of employer matches and the part made up of employee contributions. The considerations for the employer match part would be exactly the same as the considerations for moving profit-sharing assets. One way to move profit-sharing or employer 401(k) contribution funds would be for the plan's fiduciary unilaterally to decide to do so. The problem here is that the funds in either plan are invested in a diversified portfolio, while in the ESOP they will be in a single investment. If that investment does poorly, or even fails to do as well as a prudently created portfolio would, the fiduciary may be sued for misusing employee assets. For employee deferral funds, this unilateral decision is far too risky for a fiduciary to make.

To avoid this fiduciary risk, some companies give employees a choice about whether to move some or all of their account balances into the ESOP. The first potential problem this creates is that not enough funds may be moved. The second is that the employees are making an investment decision in doing this. Securities law is unclear on whether this requires a registration if the various securities law exemptions (most commonly offering less than 15% of equity) are not met, although it does appear that a one-time-only offering may be excluded. Even if registration is not required, however, full and objective financial disclosure certainly is. That can be an expensive process. It also requires the disclosure of executive salaries and other data the company may not want to make available. Finally, there is an issue about whether it is advisable, even by means of holding an election, to encourage employees to move diversified assets into company stock, especially if those diversified assets represent a significant part of their retirement.

Most ESOP advisors, therefore, recommend that at most 15% to 30% of profit-sharing assets or employer contributions to a 401(k) be moved to an ESOP by a fiduciary, and then only with appropriate advice from independent financial experts certifying that the ESOP is a good investment. Where employees are making the choice, the percentage can be much larger, but most advisors urge companies to limit the percentage employees can move except in very unusual circumstances.

Conclusion

ESOP financing is really not all that different from any kind of corporate financing. All the same techniques can be used. Unlike conventional financing, however, ESOPs can add the unique tax benefit of allowing borrowers to deduct the principal on the loan, something that can be done no other way. A $5 million loan might normally require a company to generate around $8 million in pretax earnings to repay the principal; an ESOP only requires $5 million. In return for this special benefit, however, ESOPs must meet specific rules to assure the plan operates for the benefit of plan participants. This will add complexity to the transaction, but with the advice of experienced professionals, most companies that are willing to share ownership broadly and that have solid financial prospects will find practical ways to finance their plans.

Chapter 7

ESOP Distribution and Diversification Rules

Scott Rodrick

Distributing ESOP benefits is a central responsibility and function of the plan, and it raises many issues. There are a number of interlocking rules that apply to various facets of distributions. This chapter covers the main rules. It also covers diversification, which offers ESOP participants nearing retirement the opportunity to diversify their ESOP investment by moving part of their account balance out of company stock; one way this can be accomplished is by distributing the amount to be diversified.

Companies have a certain amount of flexibility in how they may structure their distribution policies and may be more generous than the law demands them to be (for example, not delaying distributions as long as is legally permissible). However, it is important to remember that the ESOP plan document (which must adhere to the rules, such as those set forth here) controls, and that if the plan document does not authorize a particular thing the company wants to do with respect to distribution, then the company cannot do it. Therefore, the company and its ESOP attorney (and possibly other consultants) should discuss these matters and make the appropriate

---

The author thanks Karen Ng of Nixon Peabody LLP for her assistance in preparing this chapter.

plan design decisions before the ESOP attorney drafts the plan and the company establishes its ESOP. A company may modify at least some of the distribution options in a nondiscriminatory manner (e.g., it cannot treat similarly situated participants in a different manner), but it is not always clear what is permissible.

The Special ESOP Rules

ESOP benefits are mainly paid to participants after their employment with the company terminates, whether because of retirement or other reasons. There are two sets of rules that govern the main ESOP distribution issues: the special ESOP rules and the general rules that apply to all qualified plans such as ESOPs. Section 409(o) of the Internal Revenue Code (the "Code"), enacted in 1986, sets forth the special ESOP rules, which apply to distributions attributable to stock acquired by the ESOP after 1986.

Retirement, Death, or Disability vs. Other Terminations

As far as how soon benefits are paid, the special ESOP rules distinguish between *retiring* (or death or disability) on the one hand, and simply *leaving* the company due to other reasons (such as quitting or being fired) on the other hand. When a participant attains the normal retirement age under the plan, becomes disabled, or dies, the ESOP must begin to distribute vested benefits[1] during the plan year following the event (unless the ESOP plan document permits the participant to elect to defer receipt of the distribution). When employment terminates for other reasons, however, the beginning of distribution may be, and often is, delayed for some time. It must start no later than the sixth plan year after the plan year in which termination occurred (unless the participant is re-employed by the

---

1. Note that under Code Section 411(a), a participant must become 100% vested upon reaching "normal retirement age" as defined in the Code.

same company before then, the ESOP plan document permits the participant to elect to defer receipt of the distribution, or the rule stated below on delaying distributions of leveraged shares applies).

Lump-Sum vs. Installments

Under the special ESOP rules, distributions may be made in a lump sum, in installments, or in a combination of a lump sum and installments. Installment distributions must be substantially equal in size, must be made not less frequently than annually, and must take place over a period no longer than five years. This actually means six annual payments, not five: for example, a distribution beginning in 2021 and ending in 2026 (i.e., five years later) will have payments in 2021, 2022, 2023, 2024, 2025, and 2026. However, this five-year period may be extended an additional year (up to a maximum of five additional years) for each $230,000 or fraction thereof by which a participant's benefit exceeds $1,150,000 (as of 2020; these figures are indexed by the IRS for cost-of-living adjustments).

This means an employee may have to wait a long time to receive benefits. Take someone who becomes 100% vested in his or her ESOP benefit and then quits: he or she may have to wait five years[2] until distributions begin (assuming this period is not further delayed by waiting for an ESOP loan to be repaid, as described below), then another five years of installments, and, in the case of a large account balance as described in the paragraph above, up to yet another five years to receive distribution of the entire ESOP benefit. However, most participants do not have to wait that long. A 2005 survey by the NCEO found that 93.1% of all ESOPs paid out in full within one year of death, disability, or retirement. When employment was terminated for reasons other than death, disability, or retirement, 35.2% of the companies distributed within one year, 34.5% after

---

2. I.e., the participant would wait five full years, and then distributions would begin during the sixth plan year after the plan year in which termination occurred.

a five-year delay, and 25.4% after a delay of between one and five years (a handful of companies used some other approach, so these percentages do not add up to 100%).

Delaying Distributions of Leveraged Shares

Notwithstanding the above rules, the special ESOP rules provide that a leveraged ESOP in a C corporation[3] may delay the commencement of distributions of shares acquired through the loan until the plan year after the plan year in which the ESOP loan is fully repaid. However, the general qualified plan rules may mandate an earlier distribution (see below).

If the company makes distributions in installments, and those installments have been delayed by waiting for the ESOP loan to be repaid, all the installments must be completed by the later of (1) the end of the plan year after the plan year in which the loan is repaid or (2) the date they would be completed if there had been no delay. For example, take a participant who quits in 2021 at age 35. Ordinarily, the ESOP could wait until 2027 (the sixth year after termination) to begin distribution, and then make distributions in installments over a five-year period from 2027 to 2032. However, the participant's vested ESOP benefit consists of shares bought with a loan that is not repaid until 2029. The ESOP can wait until 2030 to commence distributions to this participant, but the ESOP cannot make distributions over a five-year period and delay the final installment until 2035; instead, it must complete them by 2032.[4]

If the distribution is made in a lump sum that has been delayed by waiting for the ESOP loan to be repaid, the distribution must be made no later than during the year after the plan year in which the loan is fully repaid. For example, if the fact pattern in the paragraph

---

3. It is not clear whether an S corporation can delay distributions of leveraged shares in this manner. As of this writing, some S corporations with ESOPs have done so in the absence of IRS guidance.
4. This example assumes the plan year is the same as the calendar year.

above is changed so that the distribution is a lump sum, the ESOP could wait until 2026 to make the distribution, but it could not delay any longer than that.

General Qualified Plan Rules

ESOPs are subject not only to the above ESOP-specific rules but also to rules that affect all qualified plans.

Basic Rule

Under Code Section 401(a)(14), unless the participant chooses otherwise, the plan must begin distributing benefits no later than the 60th day after the end of the plan year in which the *latest* of the following events occur: (1) a participant reaches the earlier of age 65 or the plan's normal retirement age; (2) a participant reaches the 10th anniversary of participation in the plan; or (3) a participant terminates his or her service with the employer.[5]

Mandatory Distributions After Age 72 or Retirement

Under Code Section 401(a)(9)(C), if an employee owns more than 5% of the company, the plan must begin distributing benefits to him or her by April 1 of the calendar year following the calendar year in which the employee attains age 72. If an employee does not own more than 5% of the company, the plan must begin distributing benefits by April 1 of the calendar year following the later of (1)

---

5. The 60-day requirement poses practical problems for many companies because the ESOP valuation will seldom have been completed by that date, which means that a current valuation would not be available. Because it is generally not possible to meet the 60-day rule, the common practice has been to make a good-faith effort to meet the requirement as soon as possible thereafter. While the IRS has not officially blessed this approach, ESOP professionals report that discussions with IRS officials indicate they will not challenge it.

the calendar year in which the employee attains age 72 or (2) the calendar year in which the employee retires.[6] (Subsequent payments need to be made by December 31 of the year in question.)

Distributions After Death

Code Section 401(a)(9)(B) provides that if the participant dies *after* distributions have begun but before they have been completed, the remaining distributions must be given to the participant's beneficiary at least as rapidly as they would have been given to the participant. If the participant dies *before* distributions have begun, either (1) the entire benefit must be distributed within five years after the participant's death, or (2) distributions can be made in installments over the life or the life expectancy of the participant's beneficiary, starting within a year after the participant's death (however, if the beneficiary is the participant's surviving spouse, distributions need not begin until the date on which the participant would have reached age 72).[7]

How the Special ESOP Rules and Qualified Plan Rules Interact

When the ESOP rules and the general qualified plan rules interact, the rule that would produce an earlier distribution governs. In general, the ESOP rules tend to require distributions to be made earlier, so the interplay of the ESOP rules and the general qualified plan rules usually results in an earlier distribution than would be the case in a non-ESOP plan. For example, suppose that an ESOP's

---

6. The age threshold was formerly 70½ but was changed to 72 by the Setting Every Community Up for Retirement Enhancement Act of 2019, known as the SECURE Act, effective for those who attained age 70½ after December 31, 2019.
7. Similarly, the SECURE Act changed this age threshold from 70½ to 72, effective with respect to those who attained age 70½ after December 31, 2019.

plan year is the calendar year and its normal retirement age is 65. Sally Jones retires in 2021 at age 65, having been in the plan for seven years (since 2014). Under the general qualified plan rules, she could have to wait until 2025, which is the year after the 10th anniversary of her participation in the plan, for distributions to begin. However, the special ESOP rules mandate that her distribution begin in 2022, the plan year following the plan year of her retirement.

Sometimes the general qualified plan rules require an earlier distribution than the ESOP rules would require. For example, suppose again that the ESOP's plan year is the calendar year and its normal retirement age is 65. Fred Smith, who has been in the ESOP for 15 years, quits in 2021 at the age of 64 (and therefore does not qualify for normal retirement). Under the ESOP rules, Fred would potentially have to wait until the sixth year after that (2027) for benefit distribution to begin. In fact, he might even have to wait longer (at least in a C corporation) if in 2027 the ESOP would still be repaying a loan used to buy shares in Fred's account (see "Delaying Distributions of Leveraged Shares" above). However, the general qualified plan rules override the ESOP rules because when Fred reaches age 65 in 2022, the three conditions given above will all have occurred (age 65 or retirement age, 10th anniversary of participation, and termination of service). Therefore, Fred's distribution must start no later than the 60th day of 2023 (i.e., the 60th day after the plan year, 2022, in which the latest of those three events occurred).

Where the Special ESOP Rules Do Not Apply (Pre-1987 Stock)

Because the special ESOP rules in Code Section 409(o) do not apply (unless the plan otherwise provides) to distributions attributable to stock acquired before 1987, the general qualified plan rules control such distributions, which often has the effect of delaying them compared to distributions subject to the special ESOP rules. For example, take an ESOP that did a leveraged buyout of a company in 1986 and never acquired any more stock. The ESOP's normal retirement age is 65, and the plan specifies distributions will not take place before then. In 2003, Ann, a participant who had been in the ESOP since 1986, quit the company at age 40 and hoped to receive her distributions soon. Alas, she is still waiting and, in fact, must wait until 2028 (i.e., the year in which she reaches age 65) to start receiving distributions. Such a distribution would need to commence no later than 60 days after the end of the 2028 plan year. If the ESOP deal took place in 1987, then the special ESOP rules would apply, and Ann would have begun to receive distributions in 2009 instead of having to wait until 2028. Also note that the company could amend its plan to allow pre-retirement distributions.

Distributions While Participants Are Still Employed

An ESOP is primarily a deferred income plan that provides employees with benefits after they terminate employment. However, in certain circumstances, participants may receive benefits from the ESOP while they are still employed:

- As discussed at the end of this chapter, participants may "diversify" their accounts after a certain period and may receive cash or stock directly (however, similarly to the special ESOP distribution rules, companies are not required to offer diversification for stock acquired before 1987).
- The employer may choose to pay dividends directly to participants on company stock allocated to their accounts.
- As noted above, 5%-or-more owners must begin to receive distributions when they reach age 72.
- There are certain other circumstances in which the plan may provide for in-service distributions, such as after a fixed number of years, upon attainment of a specified age, or due to the participant's financial hardship.

Form of Distributions: Cash or Stock

An ESOP may provide that distributions will be in cash, stock, or a combination of cash and stock. Closely held companies often have concerns about former employees holding company stock, either due to matters such as selling it to third parties or, in S corporations, the possibility of either exceeding the 100-shareholder S corporation limit or having the employee transfer the shares to an ineligible S corporation owner.

ESOP participants generally have the right to demand a distribution in the form of whole shares of stock, with the value of any fractional share paid in cash (even for portions of their ESOP account that were held in cash) and can then sell that stock to anyone, except that the plan may provide that the employer and the ESOP have rights of first refusal to match any offer received from a third party for such stock.

However, if the employer is a closely held company whose charter or bylaws restrict the ownership of all or substantially all (although there is no authority for what constitutes "substantially all," it is generally believed to be at least 85%) of its stock to employees or a qualified plan, or if the employer is an S corporation, the ESOP is not required to distribute stock; instead, it can distribute cash, or the employer can require the employee to sell distributed stock back to the employer.

Buying the Stock Back from Employees

Closely held companies that sponsor an ESOP must provide a "put option" on company stock distributed to participants that allows them to demand that the company repurchase the stock at its current fair market value. (There is one exception: banks and thrifts that are legally restricted from buying back their own securities can avoid providing a put option if their ESOP participants can elect to take their distributions in cash.) At a minimum, the put option must be available during two periods, one for at least 60 days immediately following distribution and one for at least 60 days after the determination of the stock's fair market value during the following plan year.[8] The repurchase obligation (also sometimes referred to as the "repurchase liability") that the put option creates is one of the main ongoing considerations in operating an ESOP.

The company may pay for repurchased shares in a single lump sum payment or in up to six annual installment payments over a period not exceeding five years (if adequate security is provided). The company's obligation to make the installment payments should be evidenced by a secured promissory note bearing interest at a reasonable rate. If the ESOP repurchases shares on an installment basis, the company must provide security and guarantee the ESOP's promissory note. Since the company can pay the employee in installment payments over a period of up to five years, selling the stock to the company does not mean the employee will immediately receive the full amount.[9]

For public companies (those whose stock is readily tradable on an established market), there is no put option and no repurchase obligation. If employees of such companies receive stock instead of cash, they can simply sell it on the appropriate stock exchange any time they wish.

---

8. This is the general rule for ESOP qualification under Code Section 409(h)(4). Readers may also encounter references to Treas. Reg. § 54.4975-7(b)(10)–(11) and DOL Reg. 29 CFR § 2550.408b-3(j)–(k), which provide that for stock acquired with an exempt loan, the put option must be exercisable during a 15-month period beginning when the stock is distributed. The 60-day rule under Section 409(h)(4), which was added to the Code in 1978, is generally regarded as having superseded the rule in the regulations, which were adopted in 1977; however, the 15-month rule may be cited by the IRS or DOL (see, e.g., Technical Advice Memorandum 200841042 [June 17, 2008]).

9. A company may use the installment payment method because it allows it to fix the value of the shares at the time of distribution (thus minimizing its repurchase obligation if the share price is expected to rise in future years) while allowing it to avoid paying the entire sum immediately.

Timing Issues and Their Effect on the Amount the Participant Receives

The price the participant receives for his or her shares must always be fair market value, but the way in which distributions are made will affect the amount the participant receives if the company stock price is changing. In each case, the date the shares leave the ESOP is the date as of which the value is determined.

- If the participant receives an installment distribution of payments from the ESOP, the amount paid per share will be determined when the distribution is made. Thus, if the stock price is rising, every year the participant will receive more per share for that year's distribution than in the previous year.

- In contrast, if the shares are distributed in a lump sum, repurchased under a put option, and paid for in installments, the price will be determined as of the date of the repurchase, and the participant will receive a series of payments based on the value as of that single date. Thus, if the stock price goes up after the distribution, the participant will not benefit from that rising price because the stock has already been repurchased, and he or she is simply receiving installment payments on that transaction. This can be helpful to the company if its stock is rising in value and it wants to limit its liability for funding stock repurchases.

- Another way for a company with a rising stock price to limit its liability for repurchases is to create a policy that after termination an employee's ESOP balance is converted into cash, which then is invested prudently until it is paid out to the employee. The amount paid for the shares is determined as of the date the account is converted to cash.

Floor Price Protection

When a company finances a leveraged ESOP transaction by borrowing money, the debt the company has taken on reduces its value. If the ESOP was already in place, then this post-transaction price drop will depress the stock value for participants who leave and receive distributions before the stock value recovers.[10] To guard against this, the company may adopt a floor price protection agreement (also called a "floor put") that compensates departing participants for the price drop during a given period, generally by paying them the difference between the price they receive for their shares and the price they would have received but for the leveraged transaction.

Participant Consent; Automatic Rollovers

Code Section 411(a)(11) and the regulations thereunder prohibit distributions being made without the participant's consent when the present value of the participant's benefit exceeds $5,000, unless the participant has reached the later of age 62 or normal retirement age under the plan. The participant must be informed in writing of the right, if any, to defer receipt of the distribution, and must provide written consent only after receiving such information. The consent requirement does not apply to dividend distributions that are deductible under Code Section 404(k) or to distributions after the death of the participant.

A "mandatory" distribution (one made without the participant's consent) of more than $1,000 and not more than $5,000 must be automatically rolled over into an IRA unless the participant elects to have it rolled over to another retirement plan or to receive it directly. If the company does not want to deal with rollovers to IRA accounts

---

10. With a new ESOP, the stock price will probably recover by the time participants vest, build up their accounts, leave the company, and receive distributions.

without participant consent, it can require participant consent for all distributions or lower the dollar threshold for distributions without participant consent from $5,000 to $1,000.

Employee Taxes

Participants pay no tax on stock allocated to their ESOP accounts until they receive distributions, at which time they are taxed on the distributions. If they are younger than age 59½ (or age 55 if they have terminated employment), they are generally subject not only to applicable taxes but also to the additional 10% excise tax on early distributions from a retirement plan unless they roll the money over to an IRA or to a qualified retirement plan maintained by another company. (The 10% additional tax does not apply to certain situations such as termination of employment due to death or disability, or distributions to an alternate payee under a qualified domestic relations order.) Employees born before 1936 who have participated in the plan for five years are eligible for favorable 10-year income averaging on lump-sum distributions.

If the money *is* rolled over into a traditional (not Roth) IRA or another qualified retirement plan, the employee pays no tax until the money is withdrawn, at which point it is taxed as ordinary income. However, if the person is younger than age 59½ at the time of withdrawal, the rules that generally impose a 10% excise tax on early distributions will apply. If the ESOP distribution is rolled over to a Roth IRA, it is immediately taxed as ordinary income. A distribution from the ESOP is not eligible for rollover if it is one of a series of annual installments over a period of 10 years (or more), if it is a minimum required distribution after attainment of age 72 (as described above), if it is a distribution made on account of a participant's hardship, or if it is a dividend that is paid directly to plan participants.

The above paragraphs refer to money being rolled over, but if the company is a C corporation and the employee receives stock in an ESOP distribution, he or she can roll the stock over into an IRA if the IRA's trustee will accept it.[11]

When dividends are directly paid to plan participants on the stock allocated to their ESOP accounts, such dividends are fully taxable as ordinary income (not as qualified dividends), although they are exempt from income tax withholding and are not subject to the excise tax that applies to early distributions. However, S corporation distributions paid directly to ESOP participants are apparently subject to the excise tax on early distributions, although the law is presently unclear on this point.

The Net Unrealized Appreciation Strategy

When participants receive a lump-sum distribution of stock due to termination of employment or attainment of age 59½, they are not taxed, unless they so choose, on the net unrealized appreciation (NUA) of the shares—the appreciation in value of the stock while held by the plan, i.e., the difference between the value of the shares when the ESOP acquired them (by either purchase or employer contribution) and the fair market value of the shares when they were distributed. Instead, they pay tax on the NUA later, when they sell the shares. At that time, they are taxed on the NUA at the long-term capital gains rates on the value of the shares when distributed, and at short- or long-term capital gains rates, as appropriate, for any appreciation in value that has occurred since distribution. (If this is the rare case in which employees make after-tax contributions to the plan, NUA is also excluded from income for non-lump sum distribu-

---

11. An IRA is an ineligible S corporation shareholder, so S corporation shares cannot be held in an IRA on an ongoing basis without disqualifying the company's election to be taxed as an S corporation. However, the IRS has taken the position that an S corporation ESOP can make a direct rollover distribution of stock to an IRA without disqualifying the S corporation election if the ESOP document requires the corporation to immediately repurchase the stock and it does so.

tions of stock attributable to the amounts they contributed.) The cost basis of the shares to the plan (or current fair market value, if lower), plus the cash distributed (if any), is taxed as ordinary income when received by the participant (except to the extent of a "rollover" to an IRA or qualified employee benefit plan). If a participant directs the "rollover" of the cash portion of his or her distribution and/or a portion of his or her share distribution, the shares of employer securities actually distributed (and not "rolled over") are eligible for the special NUA tax treatment, but the special NUA tax treatment is not available for any shares of employer securities that are "rolled over" to an IRA or an employee benefit plan.

In contrast, if the entire distribution is rolled over into an IRA (including if stock is put into an IRA and sold while in the IRA), it will be taxed as ordinary income (when withdrawn if it is a traditional IRA, or when rolled over if it is a Roth IRA). Thus, employees, especially those in high tax brackets, whose ESOP stock accounts include a great deal of NUA may be able to save a considerable amount in taxes by avoiding a rollover and employing the NUA strategy—i.e., avoiding a rollover and taking a lump-sum stock distribution instead to take advantage of lower capital gains taxes.

This strategy is not for everyone, however. First, if the company is closely held (as most ESOP companies are) and the put option period has passed, will the company still buy back the stock without any legal obligation to do so? Second, even with a public company, what if the stock value falls between the date of distribution and the date the participant sells the stock? All the potential tax savings and more could be lost. In the end, the NUA strategy is mainly useful when the stock has greatly appreciated in value (thus increasing the potential tax savings) and either (1) the company is closely held, but the participant exercises the put option and sells the shares upon receiving the distribution or (2) the company is public, and the participant either sells the shares immediately or holds them before selling but is confident that the company's stock value will not fall before he or she sells the shares.

At any rate, the NUA strategy is inapplicable to many ESOP participants because they cannot elect to receive a distribution in shares. For example, this is generally true for participants in S corporations, where the ESOP will typically be drafted to allow only cash distributions (see "Form of Distributions: Cash or Stock" and note 6 above).

Withholding

If a distribution is eligible to be rolled over into an IRA or another qualified retirement plan but the participant does not elect a direct rollover, the company generally must withhold 20% for federal income tax from the distribution. Eligible rollover distributions do not include those, for example, that are paid as a life annuity; paid over a specified period of 10 years or more; payments of dividends directly distributed to participants; paid on account of a participant's hardship; or distributions paid because the participant reaches 72 and is a 5% owner. Such distributions are subject to 10% federal income tax withholding unless the person receiving the distribution elects otherwise.

Withholding applies only to the immediately taxable portion of the distribution, not to net unrealized appreciation (discussed above). Thus, for a lump-sum distribution in stock and cash, the amount subject to withholding is (1) the amount distributed in cash plus (2) the lower of the ESOP's cost basis in the shares or the shares' current value.

There are exceptions to the withholding rules: (1) the amount withheld must not exceed the amount of cash distributed, so, for example, a distribution in stock is not subject to withholding, and (2) if a distribution consists solely of shares and cash (not in excess of $200) in lieu of a fractional share, no amount is required to be withheld. Also, as noted above, dividends paid directly to participants are not subject to withholding.

Diversification

Under Code Section 401(a)(28)(B), after ESOP participants reach age 55 and have ten years of participation in the plan, they have the right during the following five years to diversify up to a total of 25% of company stock (minus any previously diversified shares) that was acquired by the ESOP after December 31, 1986, and has been allocated to their accounts; during the sixth year, they may diversify up to a total of 50%, minus any previously diversified shares. (For special rules governing combined ESOP-401(k) plans in public companies, see the end of this section.) A participant must be given a 90-day period to decide whether to diversify, and then the ESOP trustee has a further 90 days after the participant's 90-day period expires in which to implement the participant's request.

It is important to note that diversification is cumulative; that is, as a participant diversifies his or her account, the amount available for further diversification is diminished. For example, say that a participant starts off with 1,000 shares in the first year of diversification and diversifies 10%, or 100 shares, leaving 900 shares of company stock. In year two, 100 more shares are allocated to the participant's account, for a total of 1,000 shares. At this time, to compute the 25% available for diversification, the 100 previously diversified shares are added to the 1,000 undiversified shares, for a total of 1,100 shares. The *cumulative* amount available for diversification at this point is 275 shares (25% of 1,100), but the 100 shares previously diversified are subtracted from this, leaving 175 shares (out of the 1,000) that can be diversified.

To satisfy the diversification requirement, the ESOP may offer at least three alternative investments (other than company stock) within the ESOP, offer a transfer to another qualified plan, such as a 401(k) plan, that offers three or more investment alternatives (other than company stock), distribute cash to the participants, or distribute stock to the participants. Remember that in a closely held company, a stock distribution will be subject to the requirement that the company must offer to repurchase the shares at the then-current fair market value. Also, employees who have not attained age 59½ will be subject to the 10% excise tax on early distributions (in addition to regular income tax) if they diversify by taking a distribution of either cash or stock. A participant does not have the right to demand that a diversification distribution be made in the form of company stock (i.e., the ESOP could provide for only cash diversification distributions).

The above requirements (i.e., 25% and then 50% over the course of six years starting at age 55 with ten years in the plan) are the legal minimums: the ESOP plan document may be drafted to allow participants to diversify more than these minimum percentages and/or at a younger age. However, if the ESOP allows participants to diversify beyond the legal minimums, it appears that the "excess" amounts cannot be taken into account when determining whether the diversification requirements have been satisfied (because they are not the mandatory diversifications specified by law). Also, such excess diversifications can accelerate the company's repurchase obligation (due to cashing participants out of their ESOP shares at an earlier age than otherwise would be the case).

There is a de minimis exception to the diversification requirement: IRS Notice 88-56 provides that a participant with $500 or less of company stock in his or her ESOP account does not have to be offered diversification. (If used, this exception should be specified in the plan document.)

Finally, a different set of rules governs a public company ESOP that is combined with a 401(k) plan (a "KSOP").[12] All participants can diversify their own contributions at any time, and participants who have three years of service can diversify all employer contributions. Participants must be allowed to change their investment options; the rules cannot be satisfied by simply making a distribution.

---

12. These rules do not apply to stand-alone ESOPs, only to KSOPs.

Chapter 8

Choosing Consultants and Trustees

Corey Rosen

One of the questions we at the NCEO are asked most often is "How do I choose consultants to set up my ESOP?" There is no shortage of people claiming to have expertise in this field. All too often, we hear from companies whose advisors told them of their profound understanding of the law, only to find later they were not as expert as they claimed. Choosing well-qualified, experienced people is essential; the penalties for plan disqualification, improper valuations, inadequate repurchase obligation analyses, and other problems can be severe for owners and employees. While there are no formulas for choosing your advisors, there are some key questions to ask.

This decision about whom to hire may be made by the seller or sellers to an ESOP, the company board, management, or, in the case of an appraiser, the trustee.

Any ESOP will require, at least, a valuation specialist (unless the company is publicly traded), an attorney to draw up your plan and possibly negotiate with a lender, and a plan administrator. There may also be an outside trustee, an investment banker or financial advisor, a feasibility analyst, and a communications/participation consultant as well. Some people find the best approach is to hire a "packager," someone who can bring together a team of consultants to do each of these tasks. The packager would serve as your primary contact, making life simpler, if more costly. If you go this route, make sure that all of the people the packager is bringing in are experienced and competent.

There also are "turnkey" firms that provide all of the required services except, perhaps, valuation. For this, they usually refer the client to an appraiser with whom they work. We recommend, however, that the trustee hire a completely independent appraiser. The law requires an independent appraisal, and while this has never been specifically defined, the appraiser should be hired by the trustee, not the seller or company, and should have no existing or prior relationship with the seller or the company. If using a turnkey firm, make sure that each of the advisors is independently experienced and competent.

Providers should provide a client list that can be contacted. They should be members of the NCEO and/or the ESOP Association, a sign that they are actively engaged in the field and keeping up with developments. A record of having spoken at industry events and/or published on the topic suggests that there has been at least some vetting process as to their qualifications. Finally, ask for references from external trustees, which is another way to get a professional outside opinion on provider quality.

You should avoid providers who promise you beforehand that they can assure you a certain price, whether through the appraisal or a workaround based on deal structure elements, such as warrants (warrants are explained in the chapter on valuation). Warrants can be a legitimate and prudent part of seller financing of an ESOP, but there have been firms that have structured the imputed return on these warrants at levels that are well beyond what a prudent trustee should accept. These providers may want to charge you considerably more than alternative providers.

Finally, note that fees will vary widely. Some firms charge a success fee, a percentage of the final sale price that usually is between 1% and 3%. These are generally investment banking firms that quarterback the transaction and also look for alternative buyers.

Other providers charge flat or hourly fees. Which approach you use depends on your circumstances, but it is worth contacting multiple providers to make comparisons.

Choosing a Valuation Consultant

Appraisal firms may be hired by the seller or the board to provide advice on the likely sale price an ESOP can pay and may also provide advice on deal structure and terms. As noted above, however, the trustee hires the appraisal firm for the ESOP. The qualifications in either case are the same.

ESOP valuation specialists charge widely varying amounts. Part of the difference is the firm's reputation. If your valuation is ever challenged, that reputation may be worth paying for, even if the work performed is the same as that of another firm with a lesser reputation. Another part of the fee difference is how many people at the firm review the appraisal. More reviews may mean more accuracy.

Appraisers also vary in terms of their philosophy toward ESOPs. Different appraisers will place different discounts or premiums on majority or minority stakes, on the presence of a put option (this could increase the marketability and hence the value of shares), on the repurchase obligation (this will reduce share value), and other ESOP-specific factors. Appraisers also vary in the emphasis they place on different valuation methods, such as discounted earnings or comparable companies. Understanding these different approaches beforehand will help you make sense of the final results. There is not a single right or wrong way to arrive at a value, but the different approaches can result in values more or less appropriate to your needs and opportunities.

Because the appraisal has the most potential to raise litigation issues, appraisers should indicate whether the firm has ever been challenged on an appraisal and what the results were. The challenge may have been unjustified, of course, but this should be revealed and discussed in advance.

Choosing a Lawyer

Picking an attorney is somewhat simpler. The attorney for the ESOP is typically formally hired by the board. Boards should understand the attorney's approach to such issues as governance, ESOP structure, the role of the trustee, and how to arrange financing.

The attorney should provide a fee structure and time schedule that is realistic and comprehensive. An attorney may quote a fee that represents only initial plan design, not all the filings, filing updates, and question answering that will need to be done after the plan is written. Schedules for completion may be hard to predict, but avoid people whose time frame seems unusually optimistic—delays are almost inevitable. Finally, get a specific list of just what the attorney will do. While all will write plan documents and do the necessary filings, there are differences in how involved they will be in deal structuring and financing (such as helping to find lenders).

Choosing a Plan Administrator

Much of plan administration is record-keeping, so experience and price can be the key determinants here. Part of the administrator's burden, however, should be to perform and update repurchase obligation studies. Good administrators should have their own data banks of ESOP clients on which to base these studies. Studies that rely on too many assumptions or theories, rather than what actually happens, may be misleading. The administrator should be able to handle all your retirement plans.

Other Consultants

Some companies and/or sellers also want help with investment banking, feasibility studies, communications, or employee participation issues. Investment banking is very expensive, generally charged at a percentage of the financing secured. It is rarely necessary in the typical smaller ESOP, but in more complex transactions, such as where there is a need to bring in equity investors or mezzanine debt, investment banking services can be essential. Investment bankers make sense as well when the ESOP is only one option for transition. The need for other advisors depends on what you can do in-house.

Choosing a Trustee

Selecting a trustee for an ESOP is one of the most important decisions made before a plan is established. Trustees vote and tender ESOP shares (although they may be directed in this by management or employees), oversee the valuation of the stock, are responsible for investment of non-employer securities in the ESOP, pass judgment on the soundness of ESOP purchases, and generally are responsible for operating the plan in the best interests of employees.

The board of directors or, in some cases, an ESOP fiduciary committee appointed by the board selects the trustee.

Anyone can serve as a trustee. Typically, the trustee is either an outside institution with trust experience, most commonly a bank or trust company; an officer of the company; or a trust committee, usually made up of company officers and/or employee representatives.

A "directed" trustee does not act as a fiduciary but rather operates the plan as instructed by the fiduciaries (for example, a bank may serve as a directed trustee that receives instructions from a trust committee at the company). Directed trustees with substantial ESOP experience can provide valuable input and advice to plan fiduciaries (those in the company doing the directing), especially on valuation issues, where they are likely to have considerably more experience with vetting appraisals in detail. Directed trustees do not, however, relieve the fiduciaries of any legal liability. Furthermore, if a directed trustee believes the instructions from the fiduciaries violate ERISA or plan rules, the directed trustee must override the instructions.

Assuming the trustee does act as the fiduciary, having an independent, outside trustee provides some protection should the plan's operations be challenged. Presumably, such a trustee in this circumstance will make an independent decision without the conflict of interest an insider would face. On the other hand, an outside trustee can be very costly (a 2016 NCEO survey found that the average yearly fee for an outside trustee is $30,000, although initial transaction fees can be higher and fees for larger companies and more complex transactions will be higher as well), and the very independence of the trustee could diminish insider control in critical circumstances.

A reasonable compromise for many companies is to have an inside trustee or trust committee for normal operations but appoint an outside trustee for special circumstances that present strong conflicts of interest, such as an acquisition proposal.

Clearly, the trustee should not be someone without a good working knowledge of the law and the plan. Also, someone who is selling stock to the plan should never act as the sole trustee. The trustee should be negotiating for the best deal for participants, and such a person has an obvious conflict of interest that would be difficult to justify in court.

Possible Red Flags

Never use an investment banker or other deal advisor who makes an advance commitment to secure a certain price or a return on seller notes. That is simply not possible to do in advance in a properly structured transaction in which price and the terms of the seller note need to be determined by an independent expert. Also make sure the appraiser is truly independent, as discussed above. This is an obvious red flag for the U.S. Department of Labor (DOL).

Similarly, be careful with advisors who recommend solving valuation problems with complex structures that may be more aggressive than you (or, worse, the DOL) may be comfortable with. For example, while warrants in conjunction with a seller note can be a legitimate and mutually beneficial way to finance an ESOP note, if they are too aggressively structured, they can produce a result that is harmful to the interests of the plan and serve as a red flag for a DOL audit. If the valuation expert or other advisor suggests that a seller note be priced at a low interest rate in return for a higher valuation (because the company has less debt going forward), again be wary that while this can be entirely appropriate, there have been cases when the assumed rate of return to the company that extra money will produce is unrealistic.

Where to Start Looking

The NCEO website's Service Provider Directory is a searchable database of hundreds of NCEO members who are service providers in employee stock plans and ownership culture. While having people nearby is convenient, location should be a lower priority than other factors. Much of the work can be done on the phone, through the mail, by email, or by fax.

Workshops and conferences are another good place to meet consultants. There are now over 100 ESOP meetings and webinars annually sponsored by various groups, including an annual conference and other meetings the NCEO holds. They, as well as various publications, are also a good way to become educated before starting your plan. The best way to keep consultant costs down is to personally understand how your plan will work.

Finally, if you are an NCEO member, we can put you in touch with ESOP companies in your area. Their recommendations are usually valuable.

Chapter 9

ESOPs, Corporate Performance, and Ownership Culture

Corey Rosen

ESOPs offer a lot of tax and financial planning benefits, but they have often also been touted as a way to improve corporate performance. But do they? And what does a company need to do to make sure this happens?

It may seem obvious that if employees are owners, they will work harder, and if they work harder the company will perform better. What seems obvious is not always true, however. The story turns out to be more complex.

Consider the case of Hyperthem. Hypertherm is a 100% ESOP-owned, 1,400-employee global company that manufactures plasma cutting tools. It has doubled employment in just the last 10 years. Each year, through its team-based employee involvement system, it generates about 2,000 well-developed ideas, of which about 1,500 are implemented. Imagine if in your company, every year, you got at least one good idea, from every employee, that made your company better. How much stronger would your company be?

Hypertherm and other great ESOP companies understand that the key to successful ownership culture is employee involvement. It's really very simple:

> *The most effective employee ownership companies are the ones that generate and use the most good ideas from the most people about the most different things that can make the company better.*

Extensive research has confirmed this seemingly obvious conclusion. But as obvious as it is, a culture that not only allows and encourages employee idea generation, but bakes that process into its structure of work, is still not the norm in most employee ownership companies and is even less the norm in conventional companies.

A 2017 Gallup poll, for instance, found that only three in 10 employees strongly agree with the statement that their opinions seem to count at work. Gallup calculated that by "moving the ratio to six in 10 employees, organizations could realize a 27% reduction in turnover, a 40% reduction in safety incidents, and a 12% increase in productivity."

As Alan Robinson and Dean Schroeder write in their seminal book *Ideas Are Free*, "Every day, all over the world, millions of working people see problems and opportunities that their managers do not. With little chance to do anything about them, they are forced to watch helplessly as their organizations disappoint and lose customers, and miss opportunity after opportunity that to them are too apparent. The result is performance far lower than it should be and employees who do not respect or trust management and who are not fully engaged in their work."

Creating ownership cultures is hard work, but it is work that is essential for success.

ESOP companies do perform better than would be expected if they did not have an ESOP, but to make that happen, they need to create what we call "an ownership culture." Ownership culture companies do three things:

1. They share enough ownership on a regular basis with employees so that employees see the plan as financially meaningful.

2. They share lots of information. They communicate regularly and effectively with employees to make sure they understand how the ESOP works, usually getting employees involved in the process of communication. They also share a lot of information about how the company is performing financially both overall and at work team or other operational levels.
3. They get employees involved in making decisions about how their jobs can be performed better. That takes many forms, such as work teams, ad hoc committees, advisory groups, suggestion systems, and other approaches.

This chapter looks at how we know this and then turns to what we have found are the best practices for achieving it.

The Research

The research on employee ownership and corporate performance comes to a very definite conclusion: the combination of ownership and participative management is a powerful competitive tool. Neither ownership nor participation alone, however, accomplishes very much. The findings also seem to apply primarily to closely held companies. Research indicates that public companies generally do not view employee ownership as much more than another corporate benefit. For this and other reasons explored below, the relationship between employee ownership and corporate performance in public companies is ambiguous.

In 2000, in the largest and most significant study to date on the performance of ESOPs in closely held companies, Douglas Kruse and Joseph Blasi, both of Rutgers University, found that ESOPs increase sales, employment, and sales per employee by about 2.3% to 2.4% per year over what would have been expected absent an ESOP. ESOP companies are also somewhat more likely to still be in business several years later.

While this study showed that ESOPs performed better, it did not attempt to address why that happened. The first study to show a specific causal linkage between employee ownership and corporate performance was by Michael Quarrey and Corey Rosen of the NCEO. That study also looked beneath the results to see what seemed to cause the differences. The study looked at the performance of ESOP companies for five years before and after they set up their plans. The study found that ESOP companies had sales growth rates 3.4% per year higher and employment growth rates 3.8% per year higher in the post-ESOP period than would have been expected based on pre-ESOP performance. When the companies were divided into three groups based on how participatively managed they were, however, only the most participative companies showed a gain. These companies grew 8% to 11% per year faster than they would have been expected to grow without an ESOP, while the middle group showed little change, and the bottom group showed a decline in performance. By participative management, the authors meant a high degree of involvement in decisions affecting everyday work decisions, not employee involvement in board-level or strategic issues. These companies were also very open in communications about financial performance and other company issues.

The results of this study proved out in many subsequent studies, including a large research project by the National Bureau of Economic Research released in 2006 of ESOPs, profit-sharing, and other kinds of plans. That study concluded it is the combination of employee involvement in work-level decisions and shared rewards that makes the difference. Participation alone has not been shown to improve performance over the long term. A large number of studies show that the impact of participation absent ownership is short-lived or ambiguous. Ownership seems to provide the cultural glue to keep participation going.

Why Ownership Culture Matters

Why doesn't just sharing ownership itself matter more? The findings may be easier to understand in the context of what actually happens in a company every day. An employee-owner comes to work with a clear financial stake in the company. For some employees, this will increase their commitment. To some extent, just working harder, or more carefully, will make a difference in itself. There will be less waste, customers will be greeted more cheerfully, there will be less turnover, and there may be more actual work done per hour. In most companies, however, all of these things will make only incremental differences to the bottom line. Labor costs are only part of total costs (10% to 50% in most companies), only some workers will actually change their behavior (typically about half, partly because some people are already working as hard as they can), and the total amount of additional "incentive-driven" work that can realistically be expected is relatively small (30 minutes more a day is just 6.7% of total labor costs). In fact, we at the NCEO have done calculations of how much "working harder" alone might save in a number of companies, and typically find the bottom-line impact is only about a 1% increase.

At this point, you might be thinking, "Yes, but the real issue is to get people to work smarter." We'd take it one step further: the real issue is to get whole organizations to work smarter. Organizations work smarter when they use information better. Their people have ideas about how to make their product or service better, less expensive, or both. They create more new products and new markets. They create new ways to organize the flow of work so that fewer people can do more things with the same or less effort. To make a smarter organization, a company needs as many of its people as possible engaged in the task of thinking about how everything the company does can be done better.

In conventional companies, it is up to managers both to generate the information needed to make changes and to come up with the ideas for making improvements. Information moves up and down several layers of the organization, slowing the process of decision-making considerably.

Until recently, this conventional system of management worked acceptably. Companies had the time to develop standardized procedures and keep them in place for years. Information processing and analysis was a slow, complicated job that required special skills. It made sense to organize a company so that these analytical skills were segregated among those able to do the task, while employees were trained to carry out standard procedures developed by others.

That luxury no longer exists. Product life cycles are vastly shorter. Markets are increasingly segmented and specialized and change very quickly. Information can be received, processed, and analyzed by computers in seconds. The sheer volume of information now available is orders of magnitude larger. All this information is also now available in usable formats to many more people than before. The machine operator now knows a lot more about how that machine works than a manager did a decade ago; the customer service representative looking at a screen of information knows more about the customers than managers ever knew just a few years ago. Companies can ignore these changes and plod along, restricting decisions and information to a select group, waiting for management meetings and executive approval to make changes. But they cannot succeed this way. The winners of the next decade will be companies that have more people processing more information and making more decisions faster. These will be the companies that stay ahead of the market or even learn to shape it.

Employees are the best and most abundant source of information. They are often the ones dealing directly with customers, suppliers, machines, technologies, and each other. They have ideas and experiences that can contribute to making the company work better. But in most companies, they are given neither the incentive nor the opportunity to share their knowledge, and managers have neither the training nor the motivation to listen to them even if they do. Employee-owners have the motivation, but unless there are regular, clear opportunities to share their knowledge, it is unlikely they will do so.

What does it take to enable an employee to tell another employee or a manager that something should be changed, or that there is something they should know? First, there has to be an opportunity. Do employees even have a time and place to talk to other people? Second, there has to be an expectation that the employee is responsible for sharing ideas and information. Most employees are reluctant to speak up, or even to think in terms of making suggestions, and need a lot of encouragement. Third, management must be willing to listen. Sometimes managers behave as if they are interested but do not act on employee ideas because they feel that would undermine their own position. Fourth, employees need to know that their ideas actually get used, or be told why doing so is not practical. Finally, there needs to be a structure. Employee idea sharing and problem identification happens not because you allow or encourage it; it happens because you structure it.

For employees to be able to identify important problems and solutions, they need a clear financial understanding of the company to make these efforts even more productive. That is why almost all employee ownership companies now share financial information with employees and many practice "open-book management" or the "Great Game of Business" (an approach developed by employee-owned Springfield ReManufacturing Corporation, now called SRC Holdings). These techniques involve training employees to read detailed financial and performance data and apply this context to the decisions they make every day. Open-book management practices are one of the fastest-growing trends, not just in employee ownership companies but in business generally. As SRC Holdings' CEO Jack Stack puts it, asking people to play the business game without telling them the financials is like asking people to play a game of basketball but not letting them know the score.

The numbers at the company level provide context and a sense of ownership, but the numbers at the work level are where employees can really engage. The best companies develop and share all kinds of metrics regularly followed by work teams or operational units. Employees meet periodically to discuss the numbers, what explains the variance, and what they can do about them. Sharing the numbers is not only important for making judgments but also creates a game in which employees are winning or losing. Playing basketball would be much less interesting if only the coach knows the score.

How Can Employees Generate More Ideas and Identify More Problems?

Many ESOP companies (and companies in general) are proud to say that they are an open-door company. Open doors are great, but they won't get the job done. The truth is, almost every company says it has an open-door policy. The problem is that not many people walk through that door. To be sure, some open-door policies are mere rhetoric. Management really doesn't expect employees to stand at their door, wouldn't have the time for them if they did, and wouldn't know exactly what to do with what the employees suggested anyway. But it sounds good. And most companies are sincere. Senior leaders really do expect employees to take advantage of management's genuine interest in employee ideas. Still, very few employees walk through the door.

Why? Well, put yourself in the shoes of an employee. Let's see. Do I leave my machine or my desk to go talk to the boss? Won't that cause a problem? And if I do go, when? How do I know the boss will be there? What if I go and the boss says "We've tried that before"? Or "I'll get back to you"—but never does? Or takes credit for my idea? Or, even worse, makes a big deal about my idea to my colleagues, who now accuse me of apple polishing?

For all these reasons, open-door policies are very rarely enough to create a genuinely participative environment in which employees feel not just that they can share ideas and information, but that it is part of their job to do so. The key is not just to allow employee participation, but to structure it into work routines and expect it as part of everyone's job requirement. In such work environments, participation is not just a right of ownership; it is a responsibility as well.

Open-door policies should not be abandoned, however, even if they are not in themselves enough. When employees do walk through an open door, a few practices can help encourage others to do so. First, if managers are often tied up in meetings or other tasks, make sure there are times when management is specifically available for employees. It's not unlike college professors posting office hours. Second, make sure that any suggestions result either in a detailed explanation of why the idea might not work or, if further consideration is needed, exactly what will happen next and when—and then follow through. Third, it makes sense to try to find something in the idea that is worth pursuing, even if it is just a piece of the proposal. Finally, don't assume that management always knows best. It's worth taking a risk on some ideas management does not agree with, even just to show that employee ideas are taken seriously.

Some sobering data: in our ownership culture survey, we consistently find that managers believe employees can share their ideas and get them acted on much more than employees think they can. So don't confuse what you want to happen with what is happening. If you want employee involvement, you have to go beyond encouraging it; you need to structure it.

Creating a Structure

So how do you create an actual structure where identifying problems and sharing ideas is just the way people work? There are several key components to the structure you will need:

1. Decisions are made by people, individually or as teams, based on their knowledge and involvement in the issue at hand, not on their job titles.

2. There is a bias for getting people to share ideas and information before a decision is made. Often this will be through a meeting of those involved, but other mechanisms, such as email, sug-

gestion/feedback systems, "management by walking around," or even informal networks and conversations are important as well.

3. People are given the financial and performance data needed to make a good decision and the training needed to understand it.

4. Work processes are organized into functional teams (teams of people working in the same area), cross-functional teams (teams assembled from different areas to assess the impact of decisions in one area on another), and ad hoc teams (temporary teams formed to solve particular problems) whenever the ideas and information of more than one or two people are desirable.

5. Individuals are given as much job responsibility as they can handle, not as little as they need to function.

The emphasis on meetings and teams grows out of the belief (confirmed by research) that groups of people usually make better decisions than individuals. Group participants can bounce ideas off each other, share information, and apply critical thinking to concepts in ways that those same people, tackling the problem alone, cannot. The group dynamic also stimulates an "aha!" effect—the phenomenon of getting an idea that would not have occurred to you otherwise because something someone says stimulates a new thought. Finally, decisions made by groups tend to be more legitimate to group members and, therefore, carried out with more enthusiasm.

While each of these principles is important, it is equally important to define which issues will not be decided in a broadly participative way. These would include those matters deemed too sensitive for group consideration (compensation and firing are two common examples), issues where expertise resides in only one or two people, where there is no time to make a group decision, or, most commonly, everyday issues where decisions are obvious or not important enough to be worth discussing. Participation takes time, and while it usually results in better decisions, better decisions are not always worth the cost of making them (a team is not needed to decide which pencils to buy) or possible to consider (if a customer needs a complaint resolved right away, there shouldn't be a meeting to discuss it). Management should make it as clear as possible just which issues are open for participation and which ones are not, and why.

Structures involve ways for employees to talk to one another to identify and solve problems, and often to implement solutions. These can include functional teams, ad hoc committees, cross-functional teams, self-managing teams, idea system processes for sharing ideas remotely, and other approaches.

To make a structured process work, you need to focus on several key principles:

- Identifying problems is more important than identifying solutions.
- Identifying and implementing good solutions depends on using the right metrics.
- Responsibility should be clear. Employees should not face ambiguity about what they are allowed to discuss, resolve, and implement.
- Get the right people on the right teams.
- Create psychological safety.
- Make sure there is time to do this. "Lean" can be great, but if people feel too stressed by other obligations, they won't take these processes seriously.

Start your process with the ideas team. Ideally, the team is made up of people who are not part of senior management. They may be elected by their peers or appointed by management, but most often the team will be created through a process of some people volunteering and some people being asked by management to serve.

Teams can vary in size from two to three people to several. In multidivisional companies, there may be teams at each division level and an overall steering committee.

The charge of the team is to create and operate an ideas process. These can take many forms. The team should start by getting ideas on how to get ideas. A good place to start is by reading *Ideas Are Free* by Dean Schroeder and Alan Robinson and *The Great Game of Business* by Jack Stack and Bo Burlingham. *Ideas Are Free* is a groundbreaking book showing the power of small ideas, with dozens of examples of how companies do it. *The Great Game of Business* describes the processes for idea generation at SRC Holdings, a 100% ESOP-owned company that many believe has the best-developed, most effective system for employee involvement in the ESOP world (or perhaps any world). Steve Baker and Rich Armstrong's *Get in the Game* lays out the SRC process step by step. The team can also attend ESOP conferences to listen to how companies have created their own ideas processes and can visit nearby ESOP companies.

It is essential that ideas not just be solutions to problems. In fact, it is arguably much more important to be able to identify problems. Knowing the right problems makes finding the right solutions a lot easier. Employees need to know that a great idea can just be something that identifies an issue they do not know how to solve—but someone else may. Saying "if you don't have a solution to the problem, don't bother me" is like saying if you smell a gas leak, don't tell anyone unless you know how to turn it off.

There are a lot of different ways to set up structures. Three examples illustrate how this is done.

MSA

MSA is a 330-employee employee-owned engineering company in Michigan. After some discussion and research, it came up with a system intended to harvest ideas from the entire population of the company, and how to go about implementing the best ideas. Rather than seeking large innovative proposals, the company is seeking to leverage the adoption of many small improvements. The new process has been coined the MSA Idea Engine.

A six-person Idea Engine Committee from three locations makes up the ideas team. Team members had previously gone through some Lean training together and were best equipped to implement a process for implementing improvements. The team manages the MSA Idea Engine process of obtaining, reviewing, and steering the implementation of ideas received from within the company. That involves employee huddles, an idea board, ideas email, and a vetting process for the ideas. All employees participate in one or more teams based on their functions.

Huddles by each team in the company are held every month, and at every third huddle (quarterly) there is a goal of generating three ideas per employee. The team then has an idea vetting discussion and then votes for the winner, with each employee getting three votes. The whole process takes 20 to 30 minutes or less. The winning idea from each team is submitted on an idea card that looks like this:

MSA Idea Card

Idea	
Name	Date
What is the problem/waste?	
Why is it happening?	
Idea:	
Date implemented:	

Note that the form asks first to identify the problem. Too often companies only look for solutions, but identifying the problem is the most important step, and vital even if the employees do not have a solution. After all, maybe the team will.

The team leader then maintains an idea board of work in progress:

MSA Idea Board

	Idea Board			
Huddle day and time				
	Ideas and Progress			
Huddle steps: 1. Review metrics 2. Ideas in progress 3. New ideas 4. Celebrate!	Idea	Owner	Task	Due Date
	Follow Up			
	Parking lot ideas	Needs help that need help [unclear] Review every three months and move to in progress when a task is assigned.		Completed ideas

Parking lot ideas are those that got the second-, third-, or fourth-highest votes, and are revisited at subsequent huddles and discussed for five minutes. Ideas from outside the teams are welcome as well.

The process generates a lot of ideas, but now there needs to be a vetting process to implement them. The Idea Engine Committee can assign subcommittees and designate responsibilities if it believes an idea can be implemented. The idea generator is contacted, and often more information is sought. Subcommittees are synced with the team's schedule.

The evaluation process works on a matrix:

MSA Idea Vetting Matrix

	Number of Barriers:	
Level of impact:	Low	High
High	Implement Ideas that will be acted on because they have few barriers and high potential.	Consider Ideas to be investigated further because they have high impact potential but significant barriers.
Low	Possible Ideas that might be acted on because they have few barriers but also limited impact.	Not at this time Ideas that will not be acted on.

Ideas team leaders send the ideas that are chosen to a designated email, and a tracking system—the "idea pipeline"—is posted so that everyone can see. The pipeline shows what ideas have been submitted and what their status is.

MSA CEO Gil Hantzsch said about the process, which only recently launched, "I look forward to seeing the ideas generated by the 'group genius' of our firm implemented. Over the coming years I believe that the aggregation of many small improvements will prove to be more impactful than any one large innovation."

Radian Research

Radian Research in Lafayette, Indiana, is a 100% ESOP-owned manufacturer of metrology products, primarily for the utility industry. Radian meters are used to make sure that the power meters utilities and others use to measure energy usage are accurately performing those measures.

Radian CEO Tim Everidge was impressed with what he saw at other ESOP companies and how they were using self-managing teams to drive performance. After some experimentation, Radian settled on five teams designated by the product families of shop products, site products, lab products, software products, and customer service. The teams were staffed based on a mix of different departments, a mix of personalities and experience, and a sprinkle of product expertise. Using these criteria, selections were made from the various employees who volunteered and a few who were "voluntold."

The system has been in place for over a year and is starting to deliver important results, but it has been a learning process to get them working right.

Everidge says the issues that have presented difficulties include:

- Gathering relevant data
- Pulling in other resources when needed
- Fearing they might be stepping on toes of others
- Delegating work to each other
- Learning how to be empowered

Teams meet biweekly and record and report progress in monthly scoreboard meetings. The teams provide quarterly reports to the executive team.

In a short time, Everidge says, the teams have resolved several production issues, saving tens of thousands of dollars. For instance, knowing customer issues and who the customer is has improved the involvement and mindset of employees. That mindset goes back to their work areas. Assembly processes are being changed due to this involvement, and it is driven by the employees.

Because the teams are cross-functional, communication between departments has improved, resulting in a better team effort. Everidge says a number of areas have improved:

- Much better communication between departments.
- Greater awareness of product/service issues and exactly who is affected.

- More proactive approach to improving on quality, delivery, and cost.
- Greater feeling of involvement and knowledge of the impact of that work.
- People feel they are getting involved with issues and are part of the solution.
- Employees who do not normally see or hear about customer issues are now exposed to that information and are directly involved in finding solutions.
- Employees are showing more interest and focus on customer issues.
- There is team involvement. As the SMTs (self-managed teams) have evolved over the last year, the team members have been involved in improving the process. Each team member "owns" issues and reports on them during team meetings.

Everidge sees this as just the start. One key goal is to use the self-managing teams to improve not just existing processes, but to identify and develop new business opportunities. The team-based approach means that customers now deal not just with sales but with a group of people from all areas of the company, making it easier to zero in on the intersection of what is needed and what is possible.

One key lesson from Radian is that having people from different areas on the teams makes them more creative as well as more effective in making sure that any new ideas will work across boundaries. Of course, some teams (including at Radian) are more traditionally focused just around one work area, such as a particular product line.

Barclay Water Systems and NMR

Barclay Water Management, a 100% ESOP-owned company with employees dispersed across the East Coast, and NMR, an ESOP-owned energy efficiency assessment company, are two high-involvement companies that have the same problem—most of their workforce is in the field. To get these people involved, both companies developed web-based systems for submitting, commenting on, and tracking ideas. The ideas teams regularly send out updates and encourage participation. At annual all-staff meetings, there are opportunities to review and raise ideas.

The tracking system is meant to generate not just ideas to solve problems, but, probably more important, identifying problems. Too often people are discouraged from raising a problem if they have no solution. The tracking system is set up on a shared platform (there is specific software for this, or you can develop your own systems). The idea management platform that incorporates the following features is a kind of interactive spreadsheet. Each company has its own variant of a tracking system, but the table below shows the key elements.

Idea tracking system							
Idea or problem	Date submitted	Owner	Likes	Team to address	Reporting by team on progress	Metrics: how well did it work?	Date resolved

In the first column, someone puts in an idea or a problem with a brief explanation. That then goes out to all employees or a selected group. The "owner" is the submitter. Similar to Facebook, in the "likes" column, people who think this is an issue that is important or affects them enters their name and their comments, including if they are willing to be on a team to address it. If there seems to be enough interest (an ideas team should make that decision), then a team is set up of volunteers, plus, in many cases, some people who are assigned to it. The group then periodically reports on its progress and resolution, and shares its results with everyone.

Creating Your Own System

These examples are just that. Our book *Beyond Engagement: How to Make Your Company into an Idea Factory*[1] has many more. Key issues to consider include:

1. Getting ideas requires more than just allowing them. It requires a specific structure.
2. In creating a structure for idea generation, you will get more employee buy-in if you have an ideas team or other group of employees participate in the process.
3. Ambiguity as to what employees can decide, where they can have only input, and where they have no role other than to be informed can create cynicism and withdrawal. Map these decisions out carefully and explain why you are doing it that way.
4. Start with what will work for you and build on success. Starting with a very ambitious plan too quickly carries a greater risk of failure.
5. Incentives for ideas will work for some companies and not for others, but they always need a specific structure that leads employees to develop ideas.
6. Ideas that go beyond simple, "no-brainer" changes should be charted with indicators for who is responsible, progress, goals, metrics, and status.
7. You can have employee involvement even in dispersed workforces. Web-based tracking systems and meeting apps can make this easier.

---

1. See www.nceo.org/r/beyond.

Getting Started

So to make this happen, create an ideas team with participation from representative employees. The team can use key books such as *Beyond Engagement*, mentioned above, and *The Great Game of Business*, *Get in the Game*, and *Ideas Are Free*. The NCEO and other organizations hold conferences with lots of panels on these topics. Have the team visit nearby ESOP companies with high engagement. Once they have enough information, set something up—it doesn't have to be perfect and probably won't be. But, as at Radian, evaluate, change, and keep going. It is a lot of work, but getting more ideas and identifying more problems is what will make your business a success story.

About the Authors

Scott Rodrick is the director of publishing and information technology at the National Center for Employee Ownership (NCEO). He designed and created the NCEO's present line of publications and is the author or coauthor of several books himself, including the bestselling *An Introduction to ESOPs* (19th ed. 2020). He created the NCEO's first website in 1994 and since then has been involved with the NCEO's presence on the Internet. He is an attorney and served at the U.S. Department of Labor as an attorney-advisor before coming to the NCEO.

Corey Rosen founded the NCEO in 1981 after working for five years as a professional staff member in the U.S. Senate, where he helped draft legislation on employee ownership plans. Before that, he taught political science at Ripon College. He is the author or coauthor of many books and over 100 articles on employee ownership, and coauthor (with John Case and Martin Staubus) of *Equity: Why Employee Ownership Is Good for Business* (Harvard Business School Press, 2005). He was the subject of an extensive interview in *Inc.* magazine in August 2000; has appeared frequently on CNN, PBS, NPR, and other network programs; and is regularly quoted in the *Wall Street Journal,* the *New York Times,* and other leading publications. He has a Ph.D. in political science from Cornell University. He serves on a number of ESOP company boards and continues active involvement with the NCEO as a member of the staff.

About the NCEO

The National Center for Employee Ownership (NCEO) is a nonprofit organization that has supported the employee ownership community since 1981. Our mission is to help employee ownership thrive. We have more than 3,000 members because we help people make smart decisions about employee ownership, with everything from reliable information on technical issues to helping companies reach the full potential of employee ownership.

We generate original research, facilitate the exchange of best practices at our live and online events, feature the best and most current writing by experts in our publications, and help employee ownership companies build ownership cultures where employees think and act like owners.

Membership Benefits

NCEO members receive the following benefits and more:

- The members-only newsletter *Employee Ownership Report.*
- Access to the NCEO's members-only website resources, including the Document Library, ESOP Q&A, and more.
- Free access to both live and recorded webinars.
- Discounts on books and other NCEO products and services.
- The right to contact the NCEO for answers to questions.

To join as a member, order publications, or find more resources and data on ESOPs and employee ownership, visit www.nceo.org or call us at 510-208-1300.

Made in the USA
Middletown, DE
30 August 2021